to

_____

from

_____

date

_____

100 days

of

cultivating

KINDNESS

a devotional journal

DEAR FRIEND,

We all know that we're supposed to be kind to others, and we genuinely want to. But it's easy to get off track when we're stuck in traffic, feel like we were wronged, face loud, contradicting viewpoints, or are even criticized for our own beliefs. How does the Bible tell us to respond to our adversaries? How did Jesus treat those who criticized Him? In I Peter 2:23, it says that "while [Jesus was] being reviled, He did not revile in return; while suffering, He uttered no threats, but kept entrusting Himself to Him who judges righteously." Jesus did not argue with His critics. He did not keep a grudge or become angry with them. Instead, Jesus carried on teaching from village to village because His focus was on pleasing God, not those who had wronged Him.

So, while none of us are perfect, we are called to become more and more like the Perfect One. That means we respond with respect, we respond with love, we respond with peace, and we respond with the hope of unity in mind. If we, as Christians, started responding with this type of kindness in every situation, to every person, everywhere we go, we would stand out. People wouldn't be able to ignore the difference we'd be making in our families, our communities, and ultimately in our world. And when we do that, we become the salt and the light (Matthew 5:13-16). If we can turn kindness into something that's not just an act, but a way of life that automatically flows through us as we journey on this earth, we will be pleasing the One who showed us the ultimate act of kindness when He gave His life to redeem us.

With respect, love, peace and unity,
Dr. Tony Evans

KIND WORDS

When I was a water safety instructor many years ago, I had to do mouth-to-mouth resuscitation on a drowning victim. This involved putting my mouth to their mouth and breathing into their lungs to help them find life again.

As Christians, it is important to check in regularly with ourselves regarding how we use our mouths. Are we, as God says to, speaking grace to those who hear us? Are we speaking truth at all times? Are we demonstrating to nonbelievers that we truly care about them? Do they know, when we're sitting beside them, that we're there to help and not hurt? And when they hear us, do they recognize our words as life-giving?

Kindness is demonstrated through good words. With every breath, we have the opportunity to say words that tear down, or words that build up. Nobody is perfect. But with how we talk to others, we can show them that the goodness of God is worth discovering and enjoying. We can allow them to have a taste of God's kindness by how kind we are to them.

Let no unwholesome word proceed from your mouth,
but only such a word as is good for edification according to
the need of the moment, so that it will give grace to those who hear.

EPHESIANS 4:29

Let all bitterness and wrath and anger and clamor
and slander be put away from you, along with all malice.
Be kind to one another, tender-hearted, forgiving each other,
just as God in Christ also has forgiven you.

EPHESIANS 4:31–32

Pleasant words are a honeycomb,
Sweet to the soul and healing to the bones.

PROVERBS 16:24

Speak Kindness + truth

Lord, make my words pleasing to all who hear them.
Fill my heart with kindness so that I speak kindness wherever I go.

POUR OUT COURAGE

The word *encourage* comes from the Greek word *parakaleo*. The word simply means "one called alongside to help." When a husband opens the car door for his wife, that's *parakaleo*. When somebody is carrying a package that is obviously too heavy, and you offer to help, that's *parakaleo*. When someone is weeping, and you wrap your arms around them, that's *parakaleo*. In John 14:16, Jesus called the Holy Spirit our Comforter, or One who brings *parakaleo*.

There are times in everyone's life when we need a God we can see and touch. And the way God does that is through the body of caring believers. Like cheerleaders at a football game, sometimes our job is to clap and jump and yell encouragement for someone who needs it. The game, so to speak, could have seemed over quarters ago. But when we have the Holy Spirit on our side, we have what we need to keep hope alive.

How are you coming alongside others to help? Keep your eyes open today, and maybe God will put someone in your path who needs *parakaleo*.

I will ask the Father,
and He will give you another Helper,
that He may be with you forever.

JOHN 14:16

Encourage one another,
especially now that the day of His return is drawing near.

HEBREWS 10:25 NLT

Wait for the LORD;

Be strong and let your heart take courage;

Yes, wait for the LORD.

PSALM 27:14

Be an encourager.

God, help me to be the encourager that You have called me to be.

May I reflect You in the way I come alongside others.

STEPPING IN

In Exodus 4:24–26, God told Moses to circumcise his son as an act of faith and covenant. Moses refused, and the Bible says God sought to kill Moses for it. But Zipporah, Moses' wife, quite literally saved his hide. She took the knife and circumcised their son herself. And when Zipporah interceded for Moses in this way, the anger of the Lord turned. Moses' life was saved because somebody else intervened.

How do you handle it when you see a loved one going the wrong way? And how does God expect you to handle seeing someone headed for disaster? If Moses and Zipporah are an example, it may be that you can get to the person before God does and help redeem the situation. You can act in a way that intercedes for them. Not by picking up the phone and gossiping about it to a neighbor. Not just by pointing out the person's missteps to them. But by actually doing what they are incapable of, or unwilling to do themselves. It may just save their hide.

My brethren, if any among you strays from the truth
and one turns him back, let him know that he
who turns the sinner from the error of his way
will save his soul from death
and will cover a multitude of sins.

JAMES 5:19–20

Bear one another's burdens.

GALATIANS 6:2

**Dear brothers and sisters,
if another believer is overcome by some sin,
you who are godly should gently and humbly
help that person back onto the right path.**

GALATIANS 6:1 NLT

Be a restorer today.

*God, You are the One who restores all things.
Make me Your instrument of restoration to all who need it.*

LOOK TO GOD

While he was playing one day, a boy fell and lost one of his contact lenses. He searched through the grass for forty minutes and was not able to find it. Finally, he gave up and went to his mother. His mom searched, and in three minutes, found the contact. The boy said, "Mom, I looked for so long and I couldn't find that contact. How could you find it so quickly?"

The mother said, "We were looking for two different things. You were looking for a piece of plastic. I was looking for the hundred and fifty dollars that I spent to buy it."

When you're going through hard times, it's tempting to focus on the difficulty itself. But focusing on the hardship you are facing is not going to help you rebuild. Instead, when you are suffering, look for comfort from that which you cannot see. Since God is the God of all comfort, He is the One you ought to be looking at when you need comfort.

Are you dealing with something right now that needs the loving comfort of God? Turn to Him first. Because sometimes, He's the only thing that makes any sense.

Blessed be the God and Father of our Lord Jesus Christ,
the Father of mercies and God of all comfort.

II CORINTHIANS 1:3

When you pass through the waters, I will be with you;
And through the rivers, they will not overflow you.
When you walk through the fire, you will not be scorched,
Nor will the flame burn you.

ISAIAH 43:2

For momentary, light affliction is producing for us

an eternal weight of glory far beyond all comparison,

while we look not at the things which are seen,

but at the things which are not seen;

for the things which are seen are temporal,

but the things which are not seen are eternal.

II CORINTHIANS 4:17–18

day

4

God of all comfort, I'm sorry for the times
I've focused on only the things I can see.
Help me to fix my eyes on You in faith, no matter what.

LOVE IS YOUR LABEL

When you want to know what's inside the package of food you're buying, you read the label. When you read the label on the outside, you don't have to really go dig on the inside to find out what's there because the label on the outside is the indicator of what you are getting.

For Christians, there is to be a label on the outside reflecting God's reality on the inside. Our love should be the label that lets you know how real God is in us.

How well do you love? What about other believers that you know? What about the stranger on the street? Or the people who are unkind, or harder to love? Do you reflect God's heart for them? How is your love label doing these days?

This is not some minor concern, but the heart of the serious Christian. It's the greatest way to live, and for the Christian, it's the only way to live: to let love label you, and mark you from the inside out.

For this is the message
which you have heard from the beginning,
that we should love one another.

I JOHN 3:11

We know love by this, that He laid down His life for us;
and we ought to lay down our lives for the brethren.

I JOHN 3:16

But now faith, hope, love,

abide these three;

but the greatest of these is love.

I CORINTHIANS 13:13

My label - Love as Jesus loves.

Father, Your love is the best covering and the best way forward.
Teach me to love as You do so others will know that I am Yours.

ACCESS THROUGH JESUS

After the Civil War, a soldier was outside of the White House, crying. A boy came up to him and said, "What's wrong, mister?"

The man said, "I need to see President Lincoln, but I can't get through. I'm just a common man. But only the president can solve my problem."

The little boy took the man by the hand, and said, "Would you come with me?" And he walked right past the gate. Right past the sentry. Right into the White House. Right into the Oval Office, where he said to President Lincoln, "Dad, this man needs to see you."

See, when you know the Son, Jesus, He cuts through all the red tape. With Jesus, you have bold access into the very presence of God! If we get discouraged, one of the reasons we stay there is because we don't take advantage of the access that we've been given. It is your God-given right to draw near to Him.

Therefore let us draw near
with confidence to the throne of grace,
so that we may receive mercy
and find grace to help in time of need.

HEBREWS 4:16

Draw near to God and He will draw near to you.

JAMES 4:8

day

6

Have I not commanded you?
Be strong and courageous!
Do not tremble or be dismayed,
for the Lord your God is with you
wherever you go.

JOSHUA 1:9

Father, thank You for giving us total access to Your throne through Jesus.
Teach me to pray in that power and hope.

YOU CAN DO IT!

Have you ever seen a mother getting her baby to walk? The baby's been crawling, and now he tries to get up. His legs are wobbly. He stands for a moment, and then *bam!* He falls back down again. The mother sees that he is trying. "Come on, come on, you can do it!" When the baby hears that, he tries again. He stands, and then *bam!* He's back down again. Now, the mom doesn't say to the baby, "You dummy, you'll never amount to anything." No, she encourages the baby to keep trying, again and again. And when he finally stands—"GET THE CAMERA!"

What we should find in the house of God is a bunch of cheerleaders like that mother. People saying, "Come on! You can make it! I know you're struggling with this habit or that hang-up. I know you fell down on it again last week. But come on, we can do it! We can make it!"

Whom can you encourage today? God wants us to strengthen one another and be strengthened by them. We need to be each other's cheerleaders.

Let us consider how to stimulate one another to love and good deeds,
not forsaking our own assembling together, as is the habit of some,
but encouraging one another;
and all the more as you see the day drawing near.

HEBREWS 10:24–25

Therefore encourage one another and build up one another,
just as you also are doing.

I THESSALONIANS 5:11

**Strive for full restoration,
encourage one another,
be of one mind, live in peace.
And the God of love and peace
will be with you.**

II CORINTHIANS 13:11 NIV

_____
_____
_____
_____
_____
_____
_____
_____
_____
_____
_____
_____
_____

*Lord, it doesn't always feel natural to encourage others.
Either I struggle to love another person, or I am dealing with my own pain.
Please flow through me, and teach me to encourage others well.*

IT'S PERSONAL

My father-in-law, while he was alive, did not celebrate Christmas. He believed that, one, we didn't know for sure that it was Christ's birthday; and two, it had become so secular that it didn't carry the meaning that it should. He believed it wasn't a time to worship Christ but to exchange presents. So in his family, he celebrated the New Year.

I grew up celebrating Christmas, and I have no problem celebrating it. In my home, our kids grew up with Christmas. But we didn't try to force my wife's father to celebrate it with us, because that was against his conscience. With him, we celebrated the New Year. In other words, we didn't treat the days the same.

Accepting one another means you don't judge others based on your own personal preferences. Unless God has spoken about it—unless God has regulated it—you can't control the life of somebody else. Accepting one another means making room for differences, without judgment, so that everyone can live according to their own conscience before God.

One person regards one day above another,
another regards every day alike.
Each person must be fully convinced in his own mind.

ROMANS 14:5

Therefore, accept one another,
just as Christ also accepted us to the glory of God.

ROMANS 15:7

Now accept the one who is weak in faith,
but not for *the purpose of*
passing judgment on his opinions.

ROMANS 14:1

_____

_____

_____

_____

_____

_____

_____

_____

_____

_____

_____

_____

_____

_____

_____

_____

_____

*Father, thank You for calling us to freedom where we live hand in hand with
You. Give me the ability to be kind to others who think differently.*

NICE AND KIND

We're living in a time when it's all, and only, about *me*. Many people think that what matters most is what *I* think, how *I* feel, what *I* want. They think, *If I have to harm you with word or deed to get what I want or be comfortable, so be it.* Our culture is saturated with this kind of evil. But that is not the heart of God or part of kingdom culture.

God's own kindness is what leads us to repentance (Romans 2:4). He hasn't done to us all that He could, based on what we have done to Him. He doesn't react every time we blow it. He doesn't do us in every time we fail. His kindness is great, and His kindness is the reason we are not destroyed.

So, God expects His people to be ambassadors of kindness. He doesn't just want you to be nice; He wants you to be kind. Nice can be your personality, but kindness is your action. You can be nice just because you're nice. But kindness needs to be exercised. Kindness is niceness on public display—and that is what changes the culture.

God's kindness is intended to lead you to repentance.

ROMANS 2:4 NIV

For His lovingkindness is great toward us,
And the truth of the Lord is everlasting.
Praise the Lord!

PSALM 117:2

O may Your lovingkindness comfort me,
According to Your word to Your servant.

PSALM 119:76

God, Your kindness is an incredible gift.
May I do with kindness what You would,
by showing it to others and leading them to You.

MERCY SHOWS UP

My son sends a small amount of money every month to support a young boy overseas. A few years ago, he went to visit this boy in his village. My son met the boy's father and asked him what his dream was. The man said, "I want a new house for my family, one without a grass roof because when it rains, the water comes through the grass roof and gets everything wet." My son asked the man how much a new house would cost, and he said it would cost $300.

Well, my son stopped feeling sorry for that man, and started feeling sorry for himself. Because at that moment he was wearing $300 worth of clothes, and the things that he complained about in life could not compare to a father who longed for a home for his family. So he arranged for the man to have a new house.

Mercy relieves another person's problem. It lifts the burden. Mercy pays the price.

Everyone has the ability to show mercy, because God gives new mercies every morning. Ask Him what you can do with your extra mercy today.

The Lord, the Lord God,
compassionate and gracious, slow to anger,
and abounding in lovingkindness and truth.

EXODUS 34:6

With the kind You show Yourself kind.

II SAMUEL 22:26

When Jesus went ashore, He saw a large crowd,
and He felt compassion for them because
they were like sheep without a shepherd;
and He began to teach them many things.

MARK 6:34

ask God what you can do with your
extra mercies today.

God, because Your mercies are new every morning,
I am never at a loss for Your lovingkindness.
Show me how and where to impart mercy today.

COMPANION FARE

Because I've traveled so much with American Airlines, I have platinum status with them. This means I can get upgraded to first class, and I can have a companion who upgrades with me. On one trip, my son was traveling with me. But when they offered me an upgrade, they didn't offer one to my son. I questioned it, and after they dug deeper, they discovered why. When we bought our tickets, we didn't book them together. So even though I knew my son was my companion, American Airlines did not know.

It's not that God hasn't made provision for you. It's not that God hasn't put you in His will. But you must be willing to be His companion. You must choose to be yoked to God and His authority. If you're wondering why you're stuck in an area, consider your willingness to be humble and expectant toward God. If you're in a battle, bow low. If you've yoked yourself to a person or situation that does not honor God, get unhooked! He wants you to receive His blessing.

Take My yoke upon you and learn from Me,

for I am gentle and humble in heart,

and YOU WILL FIND REST FOR YOUR SOULS.

MATTHEW 11:29

But the one who joins himself to the Lord is one spirit with Him.

I CORINTHIANS 6:17

day

11

That they may be one, just as We are one;
I in them and You in Me, that they may be perfected
in unity, so that the world may know that You sent
Me, and loved them, even as You have loved Me.

JOHN 17:22–23

_____
_____
_____
_____
_____
_____
_____
_____
_____
_____
_____
_____
_____
_____

Lord, attached to Your yoke is the very best place to be.
I desire today to be Your companion,
falling under Your authority and receiving Your blessing.

WAVES OF LIFE

God's goal for every person is the abundant life. That's another way of talking about the eternal life that He deposits in us at the point of salvation. The meaning of the Greek word for *abundant* is something that goes far beyond what is necessary. It refers to an overflow.

Abundant life from God is life overflowing. It's more than enough. In other words, He didn't come to give you just enough so you could make it. It's not about just getting by. Abundant life is *more* than enough.

Think of the waves on a seashore. One wave rolls up, flattens, then retracts. But before it goes far, another wave rolls on top of it, reaches the sand, stops, and rolls back. Then another. And another. And another. There's no stopping the rolling waves reaching the shore because that is their nature.

God came to give you abundant life. And when that runs out, He gives you more and more. It never ends, and you will always have enough to share.

The thief comes only to steal and kill and destroy;
I came that they may have life, and have it abundantly.

JOHN 10:10

I have been crucified with Christ;
and it is no longer I who live, but Christ lives in me;
and the life which I now live in the flesh I live by faith in the Son of God,
who loved me and gave Himself up for me.

GALATIANS 2:20

Give, and it will be given to you. They will pour into your lap a good measure—pressed down, shaken together, and running over. For by your standard of measure it will be measured to you in return.

LUKE 6:38

_____
_____
_____
_____
_____
_____
_____
_____
_____
_____
_____
_____
_____
_____
_____

Lord, may I not waste an ounce of the abundant life You pour over me.
May I share all that I have with all who are in need.
Thank You for Your abundance, Lord.

LOVE IS PERSONAL

Our command from God is to first of all love Him with all our heart, mind, strength, and soul—not as an afterthought, but first. And second, to love our neighbor as ourselves. You and I have been called to participate in the concept of love. It's to be personal, not esoteric or otherworldly—beneficial, not simply organizational or governmental. It has to do with the fact that you are a person, and your neighbors are people, and we are meant to connect.

You are meant to love your neighbor. The problem today in our entitlement-minded nation is that love has become a project or a program, not a heart or a person. It's easier sometimes to put a structure in place that helps people, without the hassle of getting our hands dirty in the trenches of relationship and compassion.

God makes it very clear that love is to be an intentional and necessary part of the body of Christ. If we're not willing to sacrifice for the sake of love, then we won't be living as Christ lived and died.

Is getting uncomfortable for the sake of love something you find easy, or at least possible? What are your hang-ups with loving your neighbor?

A new commandment I give to you, that you love one another,
even as I have loved you, that you also love one another.

JOHN 13:34

Greater love has no one than this,
that one lay down his life for his friends.

JOHN 15:13

Walk in a manner worthy of the calling
with which you have been called,
with all humility and gentleness, with patience,
showing tolerance for one another in love.

EPHESIANS 4:1–2

_____

_____

_____

_____

_____

_____

_____

_____

_____

_____

_____

_____

_____

*Father, help me to not avoid inconvenience
and uncomfortable situations when I feel Your leading,
knowing that sacrifice involves some personal cost.
Lead me to love sacrificially, for Your glory.*

ANSWERED PRAYER

The Holy Spirit operates in the realm of the heart—the place where you experience things and feel things the most deeply. And that feeds the rest of you. In the heart, the Holy Spirit breathes confidence. In the heart, He demonstrates the reality of His love and existence.

When you love God first, and then you address the needs you see—the ones God opens your heart to—then God will abide with you. And when God abides with you, then you will experience a new level of presence and operation in your life. And when He abides with you because you are operating in the way He has prescribed—loving Him and then loving others—then whatever you ask you receive from Him because you keep His commandments. In other words, you will begin to see your prayers answered!

We can look to Jonah's life to see what happens when we say no to God. God gave Jonah an assignment to go to Ninevah (550 miles from where he was). But Jonah fled to Tarshish (2,500 miles in the other direction). He would rather be 2,500 miles out of God's will than 550 miles in it. Jonah didn't think the people of Ninevah deserved to be saved, so Jonah ran from the presence of the Lord. And Jonah ended up in the belly of a huge fish. But if you respond to His commands to love God, to love others, and to follow God's will for your life, He will see you and respond in kind.

If you abide in Me, and My words abide in you,
ask whatever you wish, and it will be done for you.

JOHN 15:7

So they picked up Jonah, threw him into the sea,
and the sea stopped its raging.

JONAH 1:15

If I regard wickedness in my heart,

The Lord will not hear.

PSALM 66:18

Father, I see the connection between my willingness to follow

Your commands and Your willingness to answer my desires.

I open my heart to You today, and purpose to do Your will.

GOD'S STANDARD

The Bible only says one thing about clothing: Be modest. Don't overdress or underdress. Don't call inappropriate attention to yourself and away from God. Now, once you're modest, you can pick your colors, styles, and brands. You are free to express your style, within the context of God's guideline! He wants us to experience freedom as Christians, within His context alone.

The Greek word for *accept* means to *welcome joyfully*. When we accept someone, we embrace them kindly, even though they don't do life exactly how we would do it. At the airport, you'll see all kinds of bags—soft, hard, big, small, and all colors and patterns. At the gate, there is one standard: "Your bag must fit in here." They don't care what it looks like, as long as it fits one simple direction.

Within God's standard, people can bring whatever they want. Our job is to welcome people to His standard with joy and in freedom.

He who observes the day, observes it for the Lord,
and he who eats, does so for the Lord, for he gives thanks to God;
and he who eats not, for the Lord he does not eat, and gives thanks to God.

ROMANS 14:6

Do not judge, and you will not be judged;
and do not condemn, and you will not be condemned;
pardon, and you will be pardoned.

LUKE 6:37

He who receives you receives Me,

and he who receives Me

receives Him who sent Me.

MATTHEW 10:40

_____

_____

_____

_____

_____

_____

_____

_____

_____

_____

_____

_____

_____

_____

_____

_____

_____

Father, I know that it is by Your Spirit that I display Your character.
Grow in me the ability to welcome others different from me
with joy and kindness.

AN EFFECTIVE DISTRACTION

"Don't look down!" How many times have you heard that phrase used? Any story involving a guy climbing a tree, a lady hiking along a cliff, or anyone who is afraid of heights involves the frightened person getting that advice. The problem is, when you point out the obvious—that the "down" is scary so you shouldn't look—it makes the person focus on what they're afraid of!

But have you heard stories of someone helping a frightened person through encouragement? "Look in my eyes. One foot in front of the other. Think of the reward of completing this. You can do it!"

One of the things that happens when you encourage someone is that you motivate them toward the good. When someone needs encouragement, it is most likely because they have their eyes fixed on themselves. But encouragement helps shift their focus. When you encourage, you create a positive provocation to get them moving in the right direction.

Let us consider how to stimulate
one another to love and good deeds.

HEBREWS 10:24

But encourage one another day after day,
as long as it is still called "Today,"
so that none of you will be hardened
by the deceitfulness of sin.

HEBREWS 3:13

We urge you, brethren, admonish the unruly,
encourage the fainthearted, help the weak,
be patient with everyone.

I THESSALONIANS 5:14

_____

_____

_____

_____

_____

_____

_____

_____

_____

_____

_____

_____

_____

_____

_____

*God, let my words motivate others to keep their eyes
focused on what is true, right, and good.
Show me how to encourage others in their disheartenment.*

COMPASSION IN ACTION

A Jewish man was traveling by foot when he was attacked, robbed, and badly beaten. The first person to see him was a Jewish priest, who crossed to the other side of the road and kept going. A Jewish lawyer was second, and he did not stop. The third person was a Samaritan. He was a different nationality, one that didn't get along with the traveler's kind. But he stopped.

The Samaritan allowed his schedule to be interrupted for the sake of someone in need. He was willing to get dirty for another person, bandaging wounds and lifting a stranger onto his nice, comfortable leather-saddled donkey. He spent his own money to house the traveler and get him the medical care he needed, and he even offered to pay the bill if what he had wasn't enough.

Mercy is compassion in action. In the parable of the Good Samaritan, Jesus said that your neighbor is the one who addresses needs. Not someone from your town, not someone who looks the part. It's the one who acts on behalf of others.

"Which of these three do you think proved to be
a neighbor to the man who fell into the robbers' hands?"
And he said, "The one who showed mercy toward him."
Then Jesus said to him, "Go and do the same."

LUKE 10:36–37

LOVE YOUR NEIGHBOR AS YOURSELF.

MARK 12:31

But You, O Lord,
are a God merciful and gracious,
Slow to anger and abundant
in lovingkindness and truth.

PSALM 86:15

God, give me Your heart for people.
I want to live out Your perspective on loving and showing compassion.

BLESSING
THE SMALL PORTION

When Jesus stood before five thousand men, not counting women and children—so, more like twenty thousand people—with five loaves of bread and two fish, nobody believed they would be fed.

But what Jesus did was take that portion and bless it. You may be thinking, *How could He bless just five loaves and two fish for twenty thousand people?* But He did. He blessed it, and gave thanks for it, and began breaking it up. And not only did He feed the crowd, but the Bible says there were twelve baskets left over. You know you're living the abundant life when you have life left over.

How do you know you have leftover life? Because you've got life you can share with somebody else. Jesus came to give life to you more abundantly. If you are walking His path, then your path is predetermined to be fruitful enough for you to come alongside others in your abundance.

Would you call your current life abundant or lacking? Do you find it easy to pour out to others, or do you feel exhausted?

God is able to make all grace abound to you, so that always having all sufficiency in everything, you may have an abundance for every good deed.

II CORINTHIANS 9:8

Every good thing given and every perfect gift is from above, coming down from the Father of lights, with whom there is no variation or shifting shadow.

JAMES 1:17

How abundant are the good things
that you have stored up for those who fear you,
that you bestow in the sight of all,
on those who take refuge in you.

PSALM 31:19 NIV

Lord, Your portion is the perfect size, every time.
May I bless and give thanks for every good and perfect gift from You,
trusting for more than enough.

FAMILY FIRST

First John chapter three is sometimes referred to as the love letter. What you notice right away when you read it, is that John refers to believers as family. This is so important. Love is a family affair.

What would you think about a guy who fed all the neighborhood kids while his own kids starved? Not much! You'd say he was neglecting his responsibility toward his own home. So, when God saved you and me, He said, "I want you to become part of a spiritual family—the church." And as part of this spiritual family, where God is the Father, we're the children. We all know that brothers and sisters tend to compete and compare. So in the family of God, we get to practice loving and laying down our selfishness for the good of others.

Did you grow up with brothers and sisters? What have you learned about sharing love within the family of God?

And He said to him, "You shall love the Lord your God

with all your heart, and with all your soul,

and with all your mind."

MATTHEW 22:37

See how great a love the Father has bestowed on us,

that we would be called children of God; and such we are.

For this reason the world does not know us,

because it did not know Him.

I JOHN 3:1

So then, while we have opportunity,
let us do good to all people,
and especially to those who are
of the household of the faith.

GALATIANS 6:10

_____

_____

_____

_____

_____

_____

_____

_____

_____

_____

_____

_____

_____

_____

Father, thank You for welcoming me into Your family.
May I love my brothers and sisters as You love them.

WHO ARE THE POOR?

There's no debate that we're commanded to help the poor. But not all poor are the same in the Bible. And unless you can distinguish between biblical poor and general societal poor, you'll always feel obligated or confused about whom to help.

The *unable poor* are those who don't have the capacity to move forward. A young orphan, for example, will need help. An unhoused person will need a different type of care than a single mom living from paycheck to paycheck, who will need different resources than an older man living on government assistance. The Bible talks about widows, who were the poorest of the poor at the time. Without a husband to go out and work, she would easily plunge into poverty.

We have no obligation to the *unwilling poor*: the ones the Bible calls lazy, or sluggardly. They are men and women who refuse to take care of themselves. Second Thessalonians 3:10 actually says to refuse food to anyone who won't work. The unwilling poor can actually steal our time and resources away from those who truly have a need we could otherwise meet.

Only God can help us understand whether our compassion for a particular person will help or hurt the situation. Ask God to give you clear direction when you see a need—either felt or sincere.

In everything I showed you that by working hard in this manner
you must help the weak and remember the words of the Lord Jesus,
that He Himself said, "It is more blessed to give than to receive."

ACTS 20:35

For even when we were with you, we used to give you this order:
if anyone is not willing to work, then he is not to eat, either.

II THESSALONIANS 3:10

He who oppresses the poor taunts his Maker,
But he who is gracious to the needy honors Him.

PROVERBS 14:31

day

20

God, there is need everywhere I look,
so I need help discerning Your understanding of poor.
Allow me to serve You exactly where You lead me to serve.

WEALTH WITH SURRENDER

Most of the households in America would fall into the top 5 percent of household incomes in the world. This is important, because Paul told Timothy to instruct the rich—that would be most of us, by the above statistic—not to become conceited. Now, God is not against wealth. But He is against the side effects that wealth often brings.

I was watching television, and they came on with a medicine to help you feel better. They said, "This medicine will heal you"—then they gave a warning about side effects. They said, your problem will be helped, but you need to watch out for liver failure, kidney failure, headache, and possibly death. So I'm taking something to help me feel better, but could destroy me in the process?

Wealth might separate you from friends or create an unnecessary divide between you and others who aren't in your class. This is dangerous because you're called to love your neighbor, which is anyone with a need you can meet.

As you thank God for the abundance He gives, give Him permission to point out side effects and problem areas. Because wealth with a surrendered heart has the greatest kingdom effect.

Remember the LORD your God,
for it is He who is giving you power
to make wealth, that He may confirm His covenant
which He swore to your fathers, as it is this day.

DEUTERONOMY 8:18

He who loves money will not be satisfied with money,
nor he who loves abundance with its income. This too is vanity.

ECCLESIASTES 5:10

The LORD will open for you His good storehouse,
the heavens, to give rain to your land in its season
and to bless all the work of your hand.

DEUTERONOMY 28:12

Bless the work of my hands. I pray

Lord, thank You for every good thing that You've given. It all belongs to You.
May I steward it well, no matter how much You give.

MONITORED FOR MERCY

Sometimes when you call a company on the phone, you hear the message, "This call may be monitored for quality assurance." That means there is someone listening to see if customer service is being offered and if your problem is being addressed appropriately.

When God says, "Blessed are the merciful, for they will receive mercy," it's another way of saying, "I'm monitoring you. I'm watching to see the mercy you show to others, so that I can give you mercy in return." If you address the need for mercy in other people, then God is in a position to show you mercy when you need it.

You can't relieve everybody's trouble. But God will give you plenty of opportunity to relieve, reduce, or remove the burden someone else is carrying. When you do, you're serving a neighbor. And God will see. It will bless His heart, and when the time comes, He will bless you back.

Blessed are the merciful,
for they shall receive mercy.

MATTHEW 5:7

The Lord is not slow about His promise,
as some count slowness, but is patient toward you,
not wishing for any to perish but for all to come to repentance.

II PETER 3:9

As those who have been chosen of God,
holy and beloved, put on a heart of compassion,
kindness, humility, gentleness and patience.

COLOSSIANS 3:12

Lord, You call us to the highest standard, but not without reward.
I welcome the opportunity to show mercy to those who need it.

VERTICAL/HORIZONTAL

In Luke 12:28, a teacher of the Law asked Jesus what the most important commandment was. His answer had two parts: first, to love God with all you've got; and second, to love your neighbor as yourself. Order is always important, so loving God is the most important. But the second command is like it. In other words, you can't fulfill the second and skip the first.

The first commandment has to do with the vertical relationship between us and the Lord. The second commandment has to do with the horizontal relationship between us and others. Jesus tells the teacher that if he does both of those things, then he will live. Wait, you say: Isn't the teacher alive already? Yes, of course. But Jesus is addressing eternal life.

In order to fulfill abundant life, the life that Jesus gives, we have two calls. We need to focus first on our relationship with God, but we can't fully live that out without also loving others.

What is easier for you: caring about people, or caring about God? How do you prioritize both of those relationships in your life?

Jesus answered, "The foremost is, 'HEAR, O ISRAEL! The LORD OUR GOD IS ONE LORD; AND YOU SHALL LOVE THE LORD YOUR GOD WITH ALL YOUR HEART, AND WITH ALL YOUR SOUL, AND WITH ALL YOUR MIND, AND WITH ALL YOUR STRENGTH.' The second is this, 'YOU SHALL LOVE YOUR NEIGHBOR AS YOURSELF.' There is no other commandment greater than these."

MARK 12:29–31

The thief comes only to steal and kill and destroy; I came that they may have life, and have it abundantly.

JOHN 10:10

**If, however, you are fulfilling
the royal law according to the Scripture,
"YOU SHALL LOVE YOUR NEIGHBOR
AS YOURSELF," you are doing well.**

JAMES 2:8

_God, You have simplified the goal for us:
to love You first with all we've got, and love others too.
Your sacrificial love was the perfect example.
May I see and follow in Your footsteps._

PREQUALIFIED

Grace is all that God is free to do for you because of what Christ has done. Grace distinguishes Christianity from every other religion. Grace is the inexhaustible supply of God's goodness doing for us what we could never do for ourselves.

The good news is, God has already prequalified you. Have you ever gotten a letter from a credit card company, telling you that you already qualified before you even applied? They have already decided you're worthy of their credit. When you accepted Jesus Christ, you got prequalified. That's why you technically don't even have to ask God to bless you—once the flow of grace has been turned on, there's no stopping it. Because according to Ephesians 1:3, God has already "blessed us with every spiritual blessing." Everything that God was ever going to do for you, He's already done. Everything that's part of your inheritance in history that He plans to do for you, He's already deposited.

Grace is constant, like having enough oxygen to breathe. And it's circumstantial, coming in when you need it most, like loaves and fishes. Seek out where you need to experience abundant grace today, and ask God for His blessing.

Blessed be the God and Father of our Lord Jesus Christ,
who has blessed us with every spiritual blessing
in the heavenly places in Christ.

EPHESIANS 1:3

For it is not he who commends himself that is approved,
but he whom the Lord commends.

II CORINTHIANS 10:18

The kingdom of God is not eating and drinking, but righteousness and peace and joy in the Holy Spirit. For he who in this way serves Christ is acceptable to God and approved by men.

ROMANS 14:17–18

God, it's hard to comprehend the amount of overflowing grace You've laid out for me. Teach me to walk with my head held high in Your approval.

SERVE FOR ONE ANOTHER

When I was growing up in Baltimore, we would have crabs for dinner two or three times a month. When you put the crabs in the pot, and they start to feel the heat, they want out. So they begin to climb up to get out of the pot. But you can bank on it that another crab is going to grab the climber and pull it down. They keep climbing, grabbing, and pulling until they all have to give up.

Now if crabs were servants, then one crab could climb up and grab onto the edge, then reach back and grab another. They could push and pull each other up and out of that pot! But if nobody wants to be a servant, and everyone wants to take care of only themselves, then they'll all roast in the pot.

When the servants of God understand that's what we've been called to–to serve with love, and without attitude, with the well-being of the other in mind–then the church becomes this dynamic force that is transformative in nature.

Then He poured water into the basin,
and began to wash the disciples' feet and
to wipe them with the towel with which He was girded.

JOHN 13:5

In everything I showed you that by working hard in this manner
you must help the weak and remember the words of the Lord Jesus,
that He Himself said, "It is more blessed to give than to receive."

ACTS 20:35

**For God is not unjust so as to forget your work
and the love which you have shown toward
His name, in having ministered and
in still ministering to the saints.**

HEBREWS 6:10

---

*Lord, I want to be the kind of person who reaches back to lift others up.
Teach me to serve selflessly and without attitude
for the well-being of others.*

EDIFY ONE ANOTHER

Most of us have seen a building being imploded on television. Usually, the building is old and dilapidated, and it is taken down because the space has been allocated for something new and different. For an implosion, dynamite is strategically placed inside the building to cause it to explode from the inside out. It only takes a few seconds to level something that took a long time to construct.

Unfortunately, people have the ability to implode one another. We have the capacity to destroy each other's lives and quickly bring down what it may have taken years to build up.

But the Bible is clear that in the environment of God's family, we are to be construction workers. We should be building something, not tearing it down. The family of God should be enhancing and developing the lives of those around us, under God, not stripping and destroying them. The word the Bible uses for this is *edification*.

Our words, actions, and attitudes all have the power to build up or destroy. And God is clear that we should be using those tools to edify one another.

Let us therefore make every effort to do
what leads to peace and to mutual edification.
ROMANS 14:19 NIV

Therefore encourage one another and build up one another,
just as you also are doing.
I THESSALONIANS 5:11

But speaking the truth in love,
we are to grow up in all aspects into Him
who is the head, even Christ, from whom the
whole body, being fitted and held together by
what every joint supplies, according to the proper
working of each individual part, causes the growth
of the body for the building up of itself in love.

EPHESIANS 4:15–16

God, You are the Master construction worker in our lives.
As I apprentice with You, search my heart to only say, do,
and think things that will build up those around me.

GOD'S TRADEMARK

Designers are known by their trademarks or logos. You know Apple, for example, because of the mark that identifies it. When you shop, you recognize brand names by their labels. These are identifications that let you know the uniqueness of the product or company.

Even our own bodies have birthmarks. We have characteristics that have been uniquely placed in our DNA, starting with our own fingerprints.

God has a designer trademark, too. And those who are associated with Him are to wear that trademark so there is no question about who you are. It's not carrying your Bible under your arm or using fancy language to make yourself sound more spiritual. It isn't even showing up at church on Sunday. In John chapter thirteen, Jesus gathered His disciples together in an upper room to give them His final message prior to His death, resurrection, and ascension, and in that room, He revealed His trademark. It was love.

By this all men will know that you are My disciples,

if you have love for one another.

JOHN 13:35

You shall love your neighbor as yourself.

MARK 12:31

**A new commandment I give to you,
that you love one another,
even as I have loved you,
that you also love one another.**

JOHN 13:34

_Father, You have given me a trademark
by which everyone should know that I follow You.
Help me to wear it well._

GIVE THANKS AND YIELD

My oldest daughter would get privileges earlier than the other kids simply because she was the oldest. One of those things was taking naps. She got to stop taking naps first because she outgrew the need.

I came home one day during nap time. When I walked into the hallway, I saw that my daughter had opened the door to the room where the other kids were. She was standing there saying, "Na-na-na-na-na, I don't have to nap. You have to nap." She was using her freedom to cause problems with the other kids! Instead of giving thanks for her privilege, she was going around telling everyone else, "You have to nap, and I don't, ha ha ha!" That's a misuse of freedom. You don't use freedom to put other folks down who are not there yet. You give them the privilege to grow out of naps, too.

If you have found freedom in certain areas of life where others around you haven't, allow them the time they need to mature and grow. We can't rush others' progress. Just as the Lord is patient and kind with us, we must extend the same grace to those around us.

Live as people who are free,
not using your freedom as a cover-up for evil,
but living as servants of God.

I PETER 2:16 ESV

For you were called to freedom, brethren;
only do not turn your freedom into an opportunity for the flesh,
but through love serve one another.

GALATIANS 5:13

day
28

Therefore there is now
no condemnation for those
who are in Christ Jesus.

ROMANS 8:1

_____

_____

_____

_____

_____

_____

_____

_____

_____

_____

_____

_____

_____

_____

_____

_____

_____

God, thank You for my freedom in You.
Give me the eyes to see where I need to let others be themselves
and where I need to invite others into Your freedom.

REMEMBER ME FOR GOOD

The book of Nehemiah has a lot to teach us about helping others. Nehemiah is busy organizing people and things to rebuild the walls of Jerusalem. And all along the way, he's doing a lot of good for folks. Where he sees people being treated unjustly, he comes along and brings justice. He feeds and clothes people and defends property.

There is a phrase throughout the book of Nehemiah that can easily be missed. Whenever he reaches out to help someone, Nehemiah looks to heaven and says, ". . . remember me for good." Remember me, he says, talking to God. I fed some folks; remember me. I helped these people; remember me. In other words, "God, write this down. Because when my day comes, as I know it will, I'm going to need somebody to help me. And You'll be able to check my kindness record, and You'll be able to boomerang it back to me."

How is your "mercy record"? Do you do for others with the knowledge that God sees and takes note? The next time you find yourself in a position to help, say to Him, "God, remember me for good."

Remember me for this, O my God,
and do not blot out my loyal deeds which I have performed
for the house of my God and its services.

NEHEMIAH 13:14

For judgment will be merciless to one who has shown no mercy;
mercy triumphs over judgment.

JAMES 2:13

**Remember, O Lord, Your compassion
and Your lovingkindnesses,
For they have been from of old.**

PSALM 25:6

_Lord, help me to keep in mind that kindness is not lost on You.
That You are honored when we honor others in Your name._

LIFE TO THE FULL

There are a lot of people out there who are living half dead because they've been ripped off. Maybe they were robbed of their childhood because of an abusive parent. There are wives who were abused by their husbands and stripped of their femininity by the person who was supposed to love them best. There are people who are robbed every day by predatory schemes, people robbed of chances that equal opportunity would afford. These folks are walking around half dead because part of their life was stolen. They aren't experiencing all that life was meant to give.

The worst robbery of all, though, is when you've robbed yourself through sin, rebellion, or disobedience. When you make judgments against God, hurtful to others or miserable to yourself, you aren't living fully alive.

We are put on earth to live life to the full, because this is the only chance we get to do it. When we are put in position, we can also help others live again. God gives us ministry, ability, and availability, and when we say yes, we are offering the greatest gift to those who need it—including ourselves.

"For I know the plans that I have for you," declares the LORD,
"plans for welfare and not for calamity to give you a future and a hope."

JEREMIAH 29:11

You will make known to me the path of life;
In Your presence is fullness of joy;
In Your right hand there are pleasures forever.

PSALM 16:11

For God so loved the world,
that He gave His only begotten Son,
that whoever believes in Him
shall not perish, but have eternal life.

JOHN 3:16

_____
_____
_____
_____
_____
_____
_____
_____
_____
_____
_____
_____

Lord, give me eyes to see where others
have been robbed of some essential piece of themselves.
Put me in the path of those who need compassion and support.

ACCESS TO GRACE

You most likely take showers on a regular basis. And most likely, you never question whether or not there will be enough water for that shower. You know there will be enough water for your shower, for your household's water needs, and for other homes and families. For as many showers as you want to take, water will be available.

Availability of water doesn't equal a shower, though. To have a shower, a nozzle has to be turned on. You need to choose to access the water in order for you, and for those around you, to benefit from the water that's available for your shower.

God has made available all grace. But the "all grace" may be in vain if you don't access it. Because standing in the shower doesn't mean you're clean, unless you choose to access the water. You must engage God's grace in order to benefit from it.

There's enough grace for anybody who wants to benefit from it. God doesn't have favorite kids, and He is very generous. But in order to access that grace, you need to put your hand on the nozzle of abundant life and turn it to the setting of "faith."

Being justified as a gift by His grace
through the redemption which is in Christ Jesus.

ROMANS 3:24

But to each one of us grace was given
according to the measure of Christ's gift.

EPHESIANS 4:7

For the grace of God has appeared, bringing
salvation to all men, instructing us to deny
ungodliness and worldly desires and to live sensibly,
righteously and godly in the present age, looking for
the blessed hope and the appearing of the glory of
our great God and Savior, Christ Jesus.

TITUS 2:11–13

Lord, thank You for Your incredibly abundant and available grace.
May I do with it all that You want.

NOT ONLY CHILDREN

Most of us who go to church, go because we want God to do something for us. We need the Word, the blessing, the help, and the encouragement. And it's not wrong to want God to move on our behalf. But the reason God wants you to be a part of His family is not only for you. It's *our* Father who art in heaven—not my Father who art in heaven. It's a family affair.

What God has done is to place us in an extended family. At church, we learn what it's like to have spiritual brothers and sisters. In His family, no one is an only child—which means our selfishness gets tested. But also, we get to practice sharing our love, blessings, and skills with others. God doesn't want you merely to be a reservoir to receive His blessing, but also an aqueduct to convey it. He wants you to be a tool of dispensing, not merely a container of receiving.

And so, God has made this thing of horizontal love—how we touch others—critical.

How has your sense of self been affected by being a part of God's family?

For those whom He foreknew,
He also predestined to become conformed to the image of His Son,
so that He would be the firstborn among many brethren.

ROMANS 8:29

So then you are no longer strangers and aliens,
but you are fellow citizens with the saints, and are of God's household.

EPHESIANS 2:19

For by one Spirit we were all baptized into one body, whether Jews or Greeks, whether slaves or free, and we were all made to drink of one Spirit.

I CORINTHIANS 12:13

Lord, Your design for shaking our selfishness and sharing our love is perfect.
Show me exactly how I fit into Your family so that I can shine for You.

GOD-GIVEN ENJOYMENT

God isn't against having good things or enjoying His gifts. In fact, He gives us good things with the expectation that we will enjoy them.

The psalms are full of wisdom, and Psalm 62:10 is no exception. The writer says, if you become rich, don't set your heart on it. In other words, don't let the stuff you have get ahold of your affections. Because life isn't about money. He says to set your hope on God, who richly supplies us with everything to enjoy.

This is great news! Stuff is temporary, but the Giver is eternal. And anything given to us by God is meant to be enjoyed. If you got it legitimately and are using it legitimately, you can enjoy it legitimately. You don't have to feel guilty about the God-given things you have. God expects you to enjoy the good things in life, thanking Him for His provision.

As you enjoy what He has given, you will cultivate a greater sense of gratitude. People will see godly enjoyment and notice the difference in it from earthly accumulation. And it will soften your heart toward helping others see the God of goodness, too.

If riches increase, do not set your heart upon them.

PSALM 62:10

As for every person to whom God has given riches and wealth,
He has also given him the opportunity to enjoy them
and to receive his reward and rejoice in his labor;
this is the gift of God.

ECCLESIASTES 5:19 NASB

Delight yourself in the LORD;

And He will give you

the desires of your heart.

PSALM 37:4

Lord, Your desire for us to enjoy what You give us is a gift and a blessing.
Be glorified in how I view Your rich provision.

WITH RICHES COME RICHES

Paul tells Timothy to instruct the church at Ephesus to be just as rich in good works and generosity as they are in money and wealth. He says, I want them to be rich in good works. So here's an idea: The richer God makes you with money, the richer you should be with good works. If your money is going up but your good works are going down, you have now created a spiritual disconnect with God. If you are wanting to be blessed but are unwilling to be a blessing, then you're not paying attention to how God works.

The more generous God is to you, the more generously He wants to be able to move through you. And that expression is good works. Notice that He doesn't want you to *do* good works. He wants you to *be rich in* good works. In other words, those who have an abundance should have an abundance of good works also.

Consider your ratio of wealth to works. Are you comfortable with it? Has God laid out any good works for you that you have ignored or failed to recognize? How might you serve somebody today?

Instruct them *to do good, to be rich in good works,*
to be generous and ready to share.

I TIMOTHY 6:18

For we are His workmanship, created in Christ Jesus for good works,
which God prepared beforehand so that we would walk in them.

EPHESIANS 2:10

But someone may well say,
"You have faith and I have works;
show me your faith without the works,
and I will show you my faith by my works."

JAMES 2:18

Father, may my generosity toward others parallel
Your willingness to be generous with me.

LOVE IS A COMMAND

A lady wrote to her ex-boyfriend and said, "Ricky, I just want to tell you how much I miss you. I can't get you off my mind, and I'm so sorry for the breakup and I still love you. Love, Betty. P.S. Congratulations on winning the lottery."

Sometimes our motivations for love are selfish, looking to what we can gain by extending this love. But the biblical definition of love is so much different. Jesus says, "A new commandment I give to you, that you love one another" (John 13:34). So, loving someone or something can't be equal to liking, because no one can command you to like something. It is possible to *love* things or people you don't *like*.

God can tell you to love your enemies, even when you don't like them, because biblical love is a decision to passionately, righteously seek the well-being of another. It is not dependent upon emotion. Love is a badge we choose to wear every day. Kingdom love is what makes us stand out from the world's idea of only giving when there's something to receive in return.

Be devoted to one another in brotherly love;
give preference to one another in honor.

ROMANS 12:10

[Love] does not seek its own benefit.

I CORINTHIANS 13:5 NASB

day
35

We have come to know and
have believed the love which God has for us.
God is love, and the one who abides in love
abides in God, and God abides in him.

I JOHN 4:16

_____
_____
_____
_____
_____
_____
_____
_____
_____
_____
_____
_____
_____
_____
_____
_____

Father, thank You for loving me so faithfully.
Teach me to love others with the love You have for me.

GOD OF ALL COMFORT

When I had foot trouble, I first tried to self-medicate. I tried some ice. I tried some rub. I tried some chilling oil. I did the best I could to comfort myself. But sometimes pain can get so bad, and life's swelling can get so big, that you need to go to a professional.

Second Corinthians 1:3–4 says, "Praise be to God . . . who comforts us in all our troubles" (NIV). On the one hand, this is wonderful because it promises comfort. And on the other hand, it promises troubles. Trouble relates to the pain of life that comes your way as an occupant of planet earth, and even intensifies as a follower of Jesus Christ. In trouble, we need help to deal with that which is causing us to suffer.

No matter what your trouble is, God is an amazing Comforter! You may think your situation is too big, too difficult, or too shameful. But He promises comfort in ANY situation. You are NOT disqualified from comfort. No matter what, keep living. Because Comfort knows your address, and God will come alongside you to help.

Blessed be the God and Father of our Lord Jesus Christ, the Father of mercies and God of all comfort, who comforts us in all our affliction so that we will be able to comfort those who are in any affliction with the comfort with which we ourselves are comforted by God.

II CORINTHIANS 1:3–4

Even though I walk through the valley of the shadow of death, I fear no evil, for You are with me; Your rod and Your staff, they comfort me.

PSALM 23:4

For just as the sufferings of Christ
are ours in abundance,
so also our comfort is abundant
through Christ.

II CORINTHIANS 1:5

Father, there are times when I am desperate for Your comfort.
Help me to perceive it. And help me to comfort those
who need it in their times of trouble.

LIKE STICKS AND STONES

I know you've heard the old adage, "Sticks and stones may break my bones, but words will never hurt me." That's nothing but a lie! Probably every person you know has been destroyed in some way by something that was said to you. Maybe it was a parent who said, "You're never going to amount to anything." Maybe it was an employer who told you you're no good. Maybe it was a racial slur that made you self-conscious about your identity. The reality is, words do matter because the words you hear affect how you think, feel, and ultimately even act. If a judge says "guilty" or "not guilty," those words matter because they affect your destiny. If a doctor says "benign" or "malignant," those words matter because they affect your well-being.

What you say, how you say it, and even when you say it, affects whether you are building up or tearing down. Your words matter more than you know.

Let no unwholesome word proceed from your mouth,
but only such a word as is good for edification according to
the need of the moment, so that it will give grace to those who hear.

EPHESIANS 4:29

Be kind to one another, tender-hearted, forgiving each other,
just as God in Christ also has forgiven you.

EPHESIANS 4:32

**With the tongue we praise our Lord and Father,
and with it we curse human beings,
who have been made in God's likeness.**

JAMES 3:9 NIV

_Father, I confess that the way I speak to others can be so hurtful.
I want my tongue to reflect my heart, by speaking beauty
and truth at all times. Only You can do that work in me._

CONNECTEDNESS

Long ago I was hammering something and missed. That's not a pleasant feeling! I mistakenly hit my thumb instead of the nail. Right away, my finger sent a message to my brain. My brain messaged my mouth to let everyone know I'd hit my thumb, and it messaged my other hand to drop the hammer and grab my throbbing thumb to bring it comfort.

My hand didn't need a program or an encyclopedia. Out of relationship, it jumped into action and reached out to another member. And it was all because of connection.

Some people use the Bible as an excuse not to be connected. They think they need to learn more in order to be a good member of the body. But when there is connection, there is Bible built in. Is the Bible important? Yes, even necessary! But when there is connection among the members, there is response in times of need.

God wants not just your place in the pew, but your place of belonging in the body. He attributes value to that kind of connectedness.

The eye cannot say to the hand, "I have no need of you";
or again the head to the feet, "I have no need of you." On the contrary,
it is much truer that the members of the body which seem to be weaker are
necessary; and those members of the body which we deem less honorable,
on these we bestow more abundant honor, and our less presentable
members become much more presentable.

I CORINTHIANS 12:21–23

There is *one body and one Spirit.*

EPHESIANS 4:4

day

38

God has so composed the body,
giving more abundant honor to
that *member* which lacked, so that
there may be no division in the body,
but *that* the members may have
the same care for one another.

I CORINTHIANS 12:24–25

Lord, there are many who feel disconnected and purposeless in Your body.
Speak truth to their hearts, and show me how to love them into connection.

PEACEMAKERS

Did you know that in the more than four thousand years of recorded human history, there have only been 268 years without war? War is such a normal thing. War happens in the world, in the church, at work, in our homes, and within ourselves. So there is no shortage of the need for peacemakers.

Making peace consists of facing the conflict with truth. It's more than standing between two people and telling them not to fight. It involves the willingness to stand in the conflict and do the hard work. Peacemakers are compassionate, courageous, and willing to get caught in the crossfire for the sake of harmony.

Someone who is willing to be a peacemaker is someone who carries the kingdom of God. In fact, He says that peacemakers will be called His children. Are you one who plays it safe, avoiding all conflict? Or are you a peacemaker—someone who makes bold moves for His kingdom?

Blessed are the peacemakers,
for they shall be called sons of God.

MATTHEW 5:9

Pursue peace with all men, and the sanctification
without which no one will see the Lord.

HEBREWS 12:14

**If possible,
so far as it depends on you,
be at peace with all men.**

ROMANS 12:18

_____

_____

_____

_____

_____

_____

_____

_____

_____

_____

_____

_____

_____

_____

_____

_____

_____

*Lord, being a peacemaker can be so hard when everything,
and everybody, seem to be at war. But You can give me that
strength and sense of purpose. Equip me to make peace.*

WHO IS YOUR NEIGHBOR?

When the teacher of the Law asked Jesus who our neighbor is, Jesus flipped the script. He told a story of the Samaritan and then asked, of those passersby, who proved to be the neighbor?

That's a different question, isn't it? There's a hurricane in Haiti. There's starvation in Africa. There are people dying in the Middle East. There is so much need everywhere. Jesus encourages us not to ask who our neighbor is. Instead, He says, consider the person in need and ask who has proven to be a neighbor to them. The focus shifts from me and whom I'm surrounded with—to the person in need and who is willing to surround him or her.

Your neighbor is the person whose need you see, whose need you feel, and whose need you address. Every need you see isn't necessarily a need you feel. And you may see and feel a need but have no means to address it. God is faithful to lead you to those you can help. And those become your neighbors.

Have you seen and felt a need recently? Did you address it? Have you ever been in need and had someone address it in a meaningful way?

A new commandment I give to you, that you love one another,
even as I have loved you, that you also love one another.

JOHN 13:34

Truly I say to you, to the extent that you did it
to one of these brothers of Mine,
even the least of them, you did it to Me.

MATTHEW 25:40

God is able to make all grace abound to you,
so that always having all sufficiency in everything,
you may have an abundance for every good deed.

II CORINTHIANS 9:8

Lord, thank You for every time my needs have been met
through the hands of a friend. Lead me to my neighbors.

DEVELOPED FOR DESTINY

God delivered Israel from Egypt. They were trapped, and He set them free. Egypt was their prison, and God was taking them to the Promised Land called Canaan. Now, Canaan had its problems: Amalekites, Hittites, Amorites, and Canaanites. But it was still destined for Israel. To receive their earthly destiny, they needed to endure some trials.

You were saved and delivered from sin and Satan for the purpose of serving your destiny. But just like the Israelites, who had a wilderness to walk through in order to arrive in Canaan, there is a development period between your deliverance and your destiny. People would rather go straight from deliverance into destiny. But the wilderness is actually designed to develop you in preparation for that destiny. Because if you're not ready for your calling, you're going to mess it up.

The wilderness is hot, dry, and lacking in food and water. There are challenges you must face. But all of it serves to teach you how to trust God and allow your character to grow.

Blessed is a man who perseveres under trial;
for once he has been approved, he will receive the crown of life
which the Lord has promised to those who love Him.

JAMES 1:12

But one who looks intently at the perfect law, the law of liberty,
and abides by it, not having become a forgetful hearer
but an effectual doer, this man will be blessed in what he does.

JAMES 1:25

Consider it all joy, my brethren,
when you encounter various trials,
knowing that the testing of your faith
produces endurance.

JAMES 1:2-3

_____
_____
_____
_____
_____
_____
_____
_____
_____
_____
_____
_____
_____
_____
_____
_____

*Lord, thank You for the trials that serve
to prepare me for what You are calling me to.
Walk with me, and walk me through them.*

TWO HINGES OF A DOOR

When the man asked Jesus what the greatest commandment was, Jesus said that the first was to love God, and the second was like it, to love others (Matthew 22:36–40). The man didn't ask what the two greatest commandments were. But the way Jesus answered would indicate that the first wouldn't be complete without the second. Loving others is a part of loving God. It's like two hinges on a door; the door won't swing right if the hinges are out of sync.

My oldest daughter was an only child for two years until her baby sister was born. For two years, she got all the hugs, all the attention, and all the food and toys. But when her sister was born, she had to share all of this goodness. One day when her baby sister was newly home from the hospital, my older girl went into the room where the crib was and yelled at her sister! She had never yelled at us, her parents. But in that moment, the idea of loving her sister was a bit much for her to handle.

The family of God helps prepare us as He shapes us into His image. Loving God can feel like the easier part. But in the family, we learn the day-to-day details of loving others with His heart.

But as many as received Him, to them He gave the right to become children of God, even to those who believe in His name, who were born, not of blood nor of the will of the flesh nor of the will of man, but of God.

JOHN 1:12–13

You will know how one ought to conduct himself in the household of God, which is the church of the living God, the pillar and support of the truth.

I TIMOTHY 3:15

God decided in advance to adopt us
into His own family by bringing us
to Himself through Jesus Christ.

EPHESIANS 1:5 NLT

Father, teach me to love others
with the same intentionality that I seek to love You.
On Your behalf, in Your name, and with Your help.

GOOD WORKS

Good works are different from good things. A sinner can do good things. A person who doesn't even believe in God can build a hospital, build an orphanage, help sick people, be a philanthropist, or mentor kids. But only Christians can do good works.

A good work is a divinely authorized activity that benefits somebody else in need, for which God gets the glory, and for which you don't expect a return. Anyone can do humanitarian work without being motivated by God. But as Matthew puts it, "Let your light shine before men in such a way that they may see your good works, and glorify your Father who is in heaven." (Matthew 5:16). To glorify means to advertise or put on display. If I leave God out of something I've done, I've done a good thing and not a good work. In addition, it's only a good work if I do it without expecting a return.

Good works are prepared in advance for us to do, so God is already attached at the front end. If we detach Him, we plagiarize His intentions. Instead, assign Him the glory and He will recognize your faithfulness.

Let your light shine before men in such a way
that they may see your good works,
and glorify your Father who is in heaven.

MATTHEW 5:16

Give to everyone who asks of you,
and whoever takes away what is yours,
do not demand it back.

LUKE 6:30

For just as the body
without the spirit is dead,
so also faith without works is dead.

JAMES 2:26

God, give me the boldness to attribute You to every good work.
May I not waste Your intentions.

HIGHLIGHT REEL

When a football player tries out for a college team or the NFL, he has a highlight tape. What's not on that tape are the fumbles, stumbles, and misses. What is on the highlight tape is every pass he caught, every block he made, and every touchdown he scored. It's his best work only, and he can send that tape out with confidence. Somewhere, though, the school or the NFL have the whole tape. When they make a decision, they look at the whole film.

When you stand before God, He will have the whole tape—good, bad, and ugly. But there will be a highlight reel. And the centerpiece of that highlight reel will be the actions of love and mercy you shared with the body of Christ and the family of God.

So, what's on your reel?

By this, love is perfected with us,
so that we may have confidence in the day of judgment;
because as He is, so also are we in this world.

I JOHN 4:17

Then he believed in the Lord;
and He reckoned it to him as righteousness.

GENESIS 15:6

Walk in love, just as Christ also loved you
and gave Himself up for us,
an offering and a sacrifice to God.

EPHESIANS 5:2

God, may I love so much that my highlight reel is filled to bursting.
Show me where, when, and how to love today.

FOCUS

One of the most boring exercises in the world is the treadmill because you don't get anywhere. You step on, and you keep stepping on the same spot over and over and over and over again! But you persevere, because you know that your heart and body benefit from exercise.

In order for me to endure the treadmill, I do it in front of my television. If there's some sort of ball game or movie on, I can focus on that, which gives me the ability to handle the treadmill. See, my affliction is the goal of minute after minute, over and over. But if I can focus on watching television, it doesn't change the treadmill, but it affects my ability to keep going.

When you focus on the God of all comfort, it doesn't necessarily remove your affliction, but it gives you the capacity to keep going until the circumstance changes. Focusing on God takes you out of focusing on where you are, to who He is.

Therefore if you have been raised up with Christ,
keep seeking the things above, where Christ is,
seated at the right hand of God.

COLOSSIANS 3:1

The steadfast of mind
You will keep in perfect peace,
Because he trusts in You.

ISAIAH 26:3

You will seek Me and find Me
when you search for Me
with all your heart.

JEREMIAH 29:13

_____
_____
_____
_____
_____
_____
_____
_____
_____
_____
_____
_____
_____
_____
_____
_____
_____

Father, You are worthy of my attention at all times—
especially when I'm experiencing trouble.
Thank You for drawing near to me whenever I draw near to You.

TRUTH AND LOVE

The Bible says that when we communicate with each other as Christians, we are to speak the truth in love. Like goalposts, our words should align between these two: speaking the truth with the other person, and looking out for their well-being.

Some people lean toward the truth, saying, "The truth is important; I'm going to tell them no matter what, even if they can't handle it, even if it's unkind." But truth without love becomes dead orthodoxy. It may be true, but there's no life in it.

Conversely, love without truth is empty sentimentalism. It's making a person feel good, but not better off. If we're not telling the truth, we're not helping a person.

If you lie to me, you're hurting me. And if you tell the truth without caring about me, I may know the truth, but I may be worse for it because I'm reacting to you rather than the information.

If we connect the truth with love, then we convey the right information with the right heart. And we build a person up. Because truth may be sharp, but love is the balm that soothes.

But speaking the truth in love,
we are to grow up in all aspects into Him
who is the head, even Christ.

EPHESIANS 4:15

Little children, let us not love with word or with tongue,
but in deed and truth.

I JOHN 3:18

Death and life are in the power of the tongue,

And those who love it will eat its fruit.

PROVERBS 18:21

Lord, You always have a perfect balance for us.
May my words fall squarely between truth and love,
so that what I say hits its mark for Your glory.

WE'RE ALL SOMEBODIES

The first time a certain gospel artist came to our church, he drove up looking for valet parking. We told him, "No, you'd better go to the parking lot." He had to go find a spot and foot it to the front door just like everybody else. Why? Because everybody is significant here.

Later, that artist told us it was a humbling experience for him. He ultimately knew that our church was the place for him to stay—the place God had for him—because it let him see the world from the kingdom view instead of the world's. I want you to know that if you name the name of Jesus Christ and believe He is Lord, then you are connected to His body. You are a somebody.

Each member of the body deserves the same care. The result is a working body! Not everyone has the same job or the same notoriety, but everybody is critical and valuable.

Are you a more well-known Christian or a hidden Christian? Which do you prefer? And how do you treat other members of the body?

God has so composed the body,
giving more abundant honor to that member which lacked,
so that there may be no division in the body,
but that the members may have the same care for one another.

I CORINTHIANS 12:24-25

So those who are last now will be first then,
and those who are first will be last.

MATTHEW 20:16 NLT

Walk in a manner worthy of the calling
with which you have been called,
with all humility and gentleness,
with patience, showing tolerance
for one another in love,

EPHESIANS 4:1–2

_____
_____
_____
_____
_____
_____
_____
_____
_____
_____
_____
_____
_____
_____
_____
_____

Lord, thank You for making me THIS part of Your body,
and thank You for making others different but equally valuable.
Help me to work well in my role and encourage others to succeed in theirs.

RECOGNIZED

Barnabas was called the Son of Encouragement because he comforted people. Judas was the Son of Destruction due to his turning against Jesus. People are sometimes called by the character they've taken as an influence. Now, you and I are children of God if we have accepted Jesus Christ as our Savior. But that doesn't necessarily mean we've taken on the character of our Father.

But to the peacemaker, they will be called a son of God because he or she has taken on the character of their Father. The Bible declares that God is a God of peace, and Jesus is called the Prince of peace. The world is full of anything *but* peace. So when we determine to bring the peace that Jesus offers—to make room for Him in the center of it all—then we will be recognized, both by God and by the people around us, as His children. People will notice something different about us, and they will see God.

Is there someone in your life whom you recognize as a peacemaker? Would others recognize you as a child of God based on your treatment of conflict and peace?

For God is not a God of confusion but of peace,
as in all the churches of the saints.

I CORINTHIANS 14:33

For a child will be born to us, a son will be given to us;
And the government will rest on His shoulders;
And His name will be called Wonderful Counselor, Mighty God,
Eternal Father, Prince of Peace.

ISAIAH 9:6

Peace I leave with you;

My peace I give to you;

not as the world gives do I give to you.

Do not let your heart be troubled,

nor let it be fearful.

JOHN 14:27

Lord, may I be recognized by others as one of Your children.

May they see You at work in conflict, bringing Your peace

and caring about the hearts of those who are struggling.

PRACTICE WHAT YOU PREACH

When you do things to help people, expecting something in return, that's called business. There's nothing innately wrong with business. Jesus encourages it. But the trick is to know what is meant to be business and what is meant to be mercy. If out of my first love for God, and my compassion for you, I help you—that's being a neighbor.

Five students were told to preach a sermon on Luke 10 for their preaching class. They were to preach for twenty minutes each, beginning at 10 a.m. The students worked hard on their presentations. Before class, the professor asked a homeless man to sit outside the door to the class—broken, beaten, torn, raggedy, with a little bucket in front of him. Well, those students did wax eloquently. They pontificated with homiletical brilliance. They were sermonically awe-inspiring. But at the end of the class, the professor said, "You all have failed! You preached a good sermon about neighbors, but you bypassed one on your way in. I wanted to see who could preach and live, not just preach."

Listen closely to your heart today, and do your best not to pass by any neighbors you see.

But a Samaritan, who was on a journey, came upon him;
and when he saw him, he felt compassion, and came to him
and bandaged up his wounds, pouring oil and wine on them;
and he put him on his own beast, and brought him
to an inn and took care of him.

LUKE 10:33–34

Love your neighbor as yourself; I am the Lord.

LEVITICUS 19:18

Owe nothing to anyone except to love one another;

for he who loves his neighbor has fulfilled the law.

ROMANS 13:8

Lord, give me the presence of mind to act

when the opportunity presents itself.

Give me the courage to say yes when others would say no.

TIMES OF TESTING

The wilderness is no fun. It's the place you never thought you'd end up in when you were dreaming about your destiny with God. But God sees it differently. It's the necessary time of testing before you arrive to what He has promised.

It's important to note that your promised land isn't problem free. In fact, it's what the wilderness time is preparing you for. When you lean heavily on God because nothing is what you'd hoped for, God is testing your faithfulness with what He will eventually trust you with.

What God tells you in the wilderness may not make sense. It may be different from what your friends tell you. It may not be what you prefer. But when you worshiped God and told Him you were surrendering everything to Him, this is the place where He tests your truthfulness—when He tests whether you believe your friends, your neighbors, or Him.

Testing times are never what we choose, but they lead to the abundance that allows us to worship Him more purely and love others more fully. Are you in a wilderness or a promised land? Do you see the benefits of both?

Trust in the Lord with all your heart
And do not lean on your own understanding.
In all your ways acknowledge Him,
And He will make your paths straight.

PROVERBS 3:5–6

For it is God who is at work in you,
both to will and to work for His good pleasure.

PHILIPPIANS 2:13

For whoever wishes to save his life will lose it;
but whoever loses his life for My sake will find it.

MATTHEW 16:25

Father, it's hard to feel blessed in the wilderness times.
Adjust my perspective so I can faithfully wait and patiently understand
that You are hard at work for Your glory and my good.

day
50

KNOWING GOD THROUGH LOVE

First John 3:14 says that "a person who has no love is still dead" (NLT). He says that anyone who hates his brother is a murderer! It's important to note that here, John is not talking to non-Christians. He is writing to Christians. He associates love with eternal life. But what is eternal life to those who are saved?

John isn't talking about everlasting life—how long you'll live in the presence of God. Eternal life in this sense refers to the quality of life, or your experience with God. You see, many of God's children don't experience the God they have access to. He is a distant stranger to them, even though they're in the family. And here's why: If you don't learn to operate on this principle of love, then you're abiding in darkness.

Love is the switch that turns the light on. Love is the key to God's house, where you can go anytime you want as one of His children. Love unites us, distinguishes us, and lights the way to our destiny with Him.

If we love our brothers and sisters who are believers,
it proves that we have passed from death to life.
But a person who has no love is still dead.

I JOHN 3:14 NLT

This is eternal life, that they may know You,
the only true God, and Jesus Christ whom You have sent.

JOHN 17:3

This is the message we have heard from Him and announce to you, that God is Light, and in Him there is no darkness at all.

I JOHN 1:5

Lord, I confess that at times I don't love well.
But I want to live in Your light, experiencing Your presence to the full.
Lead me to love well.

NO EXPECTATIONS

Do you want to know how to get God's undivided attention? First, do the good works He has prepared for you to do. Second, attribute those works to Him. And third, do good works without expecting anything in return.

Even a sinner will lend to somebody, expecting to be repaid. But there's great blessing in lending, helping, or doing something for someone else without expecting to get paid back. Love your enemies and do good, lend expecting nothing in return, and your reward will be great. Hebrews 13:16 says that if you do good and share, then it will please God. He will notice—and He will smile.

Parents are some of the most obvious examples of this. Raising a child well is a good work. It is sacrificial. From the moment they're conceived, kids take energy and attention. They need help. And if they ever pay you back for anything, it's a miracle! Really, though, parents don't parent expecting repayment. They get their reward through godly contentment and seeing their kids thrive.

What are other examples of good works around you?

Give to everyone who asks of you,
and whoever takes away what is yours,
do not demand it back.

LUKE 6:30

Do not neglect doing good and sharing,
for with such sacrifices God is pleased.

HEBREWS 13:16

Give to him who asks of you,
and do not turn away from him
who wants to borrow from you.

MATTHEW 5:42

_____
_____
_____
_____
_____
_____
_____
_____
_____
_____
_____
_____
_____
_____
_____
_____

*God, it's not the cultural norm to lend without expecting things back.
It can actually be seen as careless. Give me godly wisdom
and desire to look different from the rest of the world.*

GET YOUR HANDS DIRTY

In order to serve others, you're going to have to set up margins in your life to make it possible. If you spend everything you have on you, if you spend all your time on you, if you spend all your talent on you, then you won't have anything left to give to anybody else.

And please notice that a good work is something you do, not something you give. Therefore, God isn't simply asking for a check or a swipe of the credit card; He's asking for your time and talent. Good works may mean you need to take off your suit and put on some jeans. You may need to trade your dress shirt for a T-shirt. If you've gotten so high that you can't go low, then you've gotten too big for your spiritual britches.

Sometimes when people write a check, they think that's gotten them out of doing the work. But sometimes writing a check is a means of assuaging guilt for not getting your hands dirty. But doing the work is part of the process of doing good works.

God puts needs in front of you that you're capable of meeting. Are you seeing, feeling, and meeting needs today?

He who steals must steal no longer;
but rather he must labor, performing with his own hands what is good,
so that he will have something to share with one who has need.

EPHESIANS 4:28

Kindness to the poor is a loan to the LORD,
and he will give a reward to the lender.

PROVERBS 19:17 CSB

All hard work brings a profit,

but mere talk leads only to poverty.

PROVERBS 14:23 NIV

Lord, I know that my time is valuable,

but I don't always value it in the way You see it as valuable.

Teach me to see time, talent, and resources as tools for Your kingdom.

STAYING CONNECTED

If I were to chop off my hand and put it in another room, the fact that my hand is in the same building with my body will be meaningless for both my hand and my body. My hand loses because it doesn't get the benefit of the rest of me. And the rest of me loses because it doesn't get the benefit of my hand. I am going to be limited in my body if my hand is disconnected.

Just going to church isn't going to benefit you fully if you're disconnected from the body of Christ—the people. You can only maximize your vertical relationship with God through attachment with His body! Detached, there will be a breakdown in the flow of God's life.

You see, the Spirit is like blood flowing through the body. He transfers God's life to the various parts of the body. But if my hand is cut off from my arm, it doesn't get the transfer of life. So God moves through connection, but not just vertical connection with Him. Drawing near is essential. But so is reaching out.

But to each one is given the manifestation
of the Spirit for the common good.

I CORINTHIANS 12:7

Now you are Christ's body,
and individually members of it.

I CORINTHIANS 12:27

**For the body is not
one member, but many.**

I CORINTHIANS 12:14

---

*Father, thank You for making me one small part
of the larger body of Christ. Help me to connect well,
and not to hinder the flow of life to any of its other members.*

COMFORT CONDUITS

One of the reasons God lets us go through afflictions is for the ministry that He has for us. When we work through our own afflictions and receive comfort, we are equipped to benefit and comfort others. One of the primary ways that God comforts is by bringing comforters in.

God shows up vertically, through a connection horizontally. He uses the family of God to comfort the family of God on His behalf. So the reason He lets you go through some things is so that you will understand what others are going through.

If you are a Christian who's only concerned about *my blessing, my healing, my deliverance, my freedom*—then know that He can't use you to be a blessing for someone else. When you drop the horizontal, it messes up the vertical. Believers are meant to be conduits of comfort.

I don't know about you, but knowing this, I'd be looking for opportunities to be a comforter because God responds to our comforting others by bringing His comfort to us.

But God, who comforts the depressed, comforted us by the coming of Titus;
and not only by his coming, but also by the comfort with
which he was comforted in you, as he reported to us your longing,
your mourning, your zeal for me; so that I rejoiced even more.

II CORINTHIANS 7:6–7

This is My commandment, that you love one another,
just as I have loved you.

JOHN 15:12

**In everything, therefore, treat people
the same way you want them to treat you,
for this is the Law and the Prophets.**

MATTHEW 7:12

_God, You have designed us so well to pour out comfort
as You pour comfort into us. Bring people into my path
who need an understanding heart or a caring hug._

LOVE GOD, LOVE OTHERS

Our vertical relationship with God is intimately connected to our horizontal relationship with one another. When there is a breach in the horizontal, then there is a breach in the vertical. When the enemy can disconnect us from each other, he has also limited what we receive from God because God has intentionally connected the vertical and the horizontal.

First John 4:8 says, "The one who does not love does not know God, for God is love." In other words, if you disconnect from a brother whom you see, you cannot have an intimate experience with God, whom you do not see. The two are hinged.

The more we show kindness to others, the more we accept them despite our differences of opinion, the more we tell them the truth in love, welcome them, forgive and release them, show them grace and mercy—the more God can reciprocate with us. When we love, His love bursts out of us.

Be kind to one another, tender-hearted,
forgiving each other, just as God in Christ also has forgiven you.

EPHESIANS 4:32

We love, because He first loved us. If someone says,
"I love God," and hates his brother, he is a liar;
for the one who does not love his brother whom he has seen,
cannot love God whom he has not seen.

I JOHN 4:19–20

**And this commandment
we have from Him,
that the one who loves God
should love his brother also.**

I JOHN 4:21

56

*God, learning to love others as You do is a lifelong task.
May Your fruit grow in me, Holy Spirit, that others would see You
at work and feel Your love for them through me.*

SHARING IS CARING

One of the visible pieces of evidence that God has gotten a hold of you is your willingness to help somebody else. Sharing is no small thing, because it is rooted in the theology of the faith: "For God so loved the world, that He gave" (John 3:16). That is the message of the Gospel. God didn't just love us from afar; He shared Himself with us.

God is a God who shares. So if you are full of God, and God is a God who shares, then how can you be a self-centered Christian? That is a contradictory term.

God created a Creation that shares. The sun gives light and heat. The stars illuminate the night. He created vegetation to eat and everything that you benefit from. Every piece of cloth, every brick, every piece of wood or steel, every meal is God sharing with us.

One of the greatest demonstrations of an individual or a church filled with the Spirit is their willingness to share. How about you? Do you find sharing things hard or easy? Is there something you are holding tight to that God would have you share? What is one thing that someone has shared with you lately?

After they prayed, the place where they were meeting was shaken.
And they were all filled with the Holy Spirit and spoke the word of God
boldly. All the believers were one in heart and mind. No one claimed that
any of their possessions was their own, but they shared everything they had.

ACTS 4:31–32 NIV

And do not neglect doing good and sharing,
for with such sacrifices God is pleased.

HEBREWS 13:16

And with great power the apostles were giving
testimony to the resurrection of the Lord Jesus,
and abundant grace was upon them all.
For there was not a needy person among them,
for all who were owners of land or houses
would sell them and bring the proceeds of
the sales and lay them at the apostles' feet, and
they would be distributed to each as any had need.

ACTS 4:33–35

Lord, thank You for sharing all that You created with us.
Holy Spirit, You are invited to fill me to the fullest
so that I can share all that I have with others.

RECONCILED

When your checkbook and your bank statement don't agree, you know there is a problem somewhere. You can't have reconciliation between the two until you identify where and why the two numbers aren't the same. What you don't do is say, "I'm sure it will all work out." No, you don't skip finding the error if you really want reconciliation.

Jesus said, "In the world you have tribulation" (John 16:33). You will run into conflict, that's a promise. And while He offers peace to cover you, true peacemaking involves finding the root sin of the issue and addressing that. Do you have a very good friend or family member who will help you to identify the sin and walk you through the process of reconciliation? It may hurt for a short while, but the reward of God's peace is well worth it.

Are you willing to walk through the reconciliation process when needed? Do you lean toward healthy conflict when it comes, or do you run away?

In the world you have tribulation,
but take courage;
I have overcome the world.

JOHN 16:33

If your brother sins,
go and show him his fault in private;
if he listens to you,
you have won your brother.

MATTHEW 18:15

Therefore if you are presenting your offering at the altar, and there remember that your brother has something against you, leave your offering there before the altar and go; first be reconciled to your brother, and then come and present your offering.

MATTHEW 5:23–24

Father, thank You for your peace to cover us
as we walk through conflict toward reconciliation.
May I be a helper and not a hinderer through the process.

HELPING THE ONE

Elitism is the perspective that your progress from apartment to house, from the bus to a car, from Sears to Neiman Marcus, makes you better than someone who is still stuck. God is not against your progress if done biblically, spiritually, and legitimately. He is against progress that makes you think, feel, or act like you're better than others who are not where you are.

God wants you to reach neighbors, and He will bring neighbors for you to reach. He will put people in front of you who tug your heart—people you have some capacity to assist.

A father was walking along a beach with his son. Hundreds of starfish had been washed up by the tide, as far as the eye could see. Every several feet, the dad was picking one starfish up and tossing it back into the water. "Dad, why bother doing that? There are hundreds of starfish out here that are all going to die. It won't make a difference." The father said, "Son, it matters to the ones I throw back."

You can't help everybody. But if everybody helps somebody, that's a lot of somebodies.

For, behold, the wicked bend the bow,
They make ready their arrow upon the string
To shoot in darkness at the upright in heart.

PSALM 11:2

One who is gracious to a poor man lends to the Lord,
And He will repay him for his good deed.

PROVERBS 19:17

Let not a wise man boast of his wisdom, and let not the mighty man boast of his might, let not a rich man boast of his riches; but let him who boasts boast of this, that he understands and knows Me, that I am the Lord who exercises lovingkindness, justice and righteousness on earth; for I delight in these things.

JEREMIAH 9:23–24

Father, may we never become so upper class that we look down on other people. May we remain humble servants to You, meeting the needs we see and feel, and receiving our inheritance from You in return.

BREAKTHROUGH

A farmer's donkey fell into a well. The farmer had no recourse to get that donkey out, so he decided the best thing would be to bury the donkey in the well to take it out of its misery. The farmer began shoveling one scoop of dirt at a time. After shoveling for what seemed like forever, the donkey stepped right out of that well! See, what the donkey did was to step on top of the new dirt every time the farmer shoveled. He kept shaking dirt off, stomping it down, and making the ground higher and higher until the inside was level with the outside.

When circumstances are piling on top of you, shake them off and take a step. One step at a time. And next thing you know, you'll be stepping into your promised land. God says there is a perfect law of liberty that, when followed, leads to blessing (James 1:25). When you plug one plus one into a calculator, the correct answer is already set up for you inside. You bring the problem. God's law of liberty has the answer. Let Him answer your problems, and you will be blessed.

But one who looks intently at the perfect law, the law of liberty,
and abides by it, not having become a forgetful hearer
but an effectual doer, this man will be blessed in what he does.

JAMES 1:25

Man's steps are ordained by the LORD,
How then can man understand his way?

PROVERBS 20:24

Your word is a lamp to my feet
And a light to my path.

PSALM 119:105

_____

_____

_____

_____

_____

_____

_____

_____

_____

_____

_____

_____

_____

_____

God, when my problems seem like too much,
I will submit them to Your answer book. You always have a way through,
and I believe You when You say that the way through leads to blessing.

WHAT'S INSIDE

If you think of the sun, and what it means to the earth, that is God to His creation. He is light. The distinction between darkness and light is the presence or absence of love. If God is operating in you, then love is going to come out of you. If God is not operating, then darkness will come out.

If you have the flu, somebody is going to know there's a virus inside of you by the sniffles, sneezes, and flushed skin. If a woman is pregnant, that seed planted inside her will be made known by her growing abdomen that makes it visible to people on the outside. If God is alive in you, then love will make that known on the outside.

Some people have lived in darkness for so long that they don't even recognize it. They are critical, unforgiving, mean, and hateful. "I'm just being me!" they say because they don't recognize the absence of God. But choose God's presence, and the good stuff—the fruit of His presence—will come out without you even trying. Those people, who dwell in Christ, will say, "It's not me; it's God." And they won't be half wrong.

If I speak with the tongues of men and of angels,
but do not have love, I have become
a noisy gong or a clanging cymbal.

I CORINTHIANS 13:1

Love never fails.

I CORINTHIANS 13:8

Remain in Me, as I also remain in you. No branch
can bear fruit by itself; it must remain in the vine.
Neither can you bear fruit unless you remain in Me.

JOHN 15:4 NIV

_____

_____

_____

_____

_____

_____

_____

_____

_____

_____

_____

_____

_____

_____

_____

_____

God, may You find Your home in me and be content to stay.

May the parts of me that get in Your way be removed.

I must decrease while You increase.

A GOOD INVESTMENT

Many of us have a storage unit where we keep things we don't want or need right now, but we anticipate wanting or needing in the future. Some of us have a bank account where we store up savings for the future. We have retirement plans or savings accounts for our kids, storing up for future needs.

What happens if we try to withdraw from an empty account or retrieve goods from an empty storage unit? Obviously nothing happens, because there's nothing there. In other words, you can only draw from an account that has been deposited into or interest paid on it.

One of the reasons many people aren't experiencing more of God is because their spiritual accounts are empty. They haven't sown the seeds of investment into their kingdom accounts, doing the good works He has laid out for them. But when you remain future-oriented with your spiritual investments, you store up treasure in heaven that will bless you in the future.

The King will answer and say to them,
"Truly I say to you, to the extent that you did it
to one of these brothers of Mine,
even the least of them, you did it to Me."

MATTHEW 25:40

So you see, faith by itself isn't enough.
Unless it produces good deeds, it is dead and useless.

JAMES 2:17 NLT

For God is not unjust so as to forget your work
and the love which you have shown
toward His name, in having ministered and
in still ministering to the saints.

HEBREWS 6:10

_Lord, give me eyes to view my actions as an opportunity
to store the treasure of the kingdom in Your bank account._

TABITHA'S MIRACLE

In Acts chapter 9 there is a story about Tabitha, who lived in the town of Joppa. This woman was abounding with deeds of kindness and charity. In verse 37, Tabitha fell sick and died. And when they had washed her body, they laid it in an upper room. Peter was in Lydda at the time, which wasn't too far away from Joppa. So two people were sent there to tell Peter about Tabitha and what had happened, and to ask him to come immediately.

When he got to that upper room, Peter saw Tabitha lying dead, surrounded by many of the people she had helped. Peter said to her, "Tabitha, arise." And she opened her eyes and sat up.

Tabitha got a miracle. But before that, the Bible takes time to describe what a help she was to others. She made tunics and clothes for widows, offering her time and talent for good works. When she ran into a crisis that her business couldn't fix, God stepped in.

When your resources begin to run dry, turn to the ultimate Source, and rely on Him to provide.

When he arrived, they brought him into the upper room;
and all the widows stood beside him, weeping and
showing all the tunics and garments that [Tabitha]
used to make while she was with them.

ACTS 9:39

Heal the sick, raise the dead, cleanse the lepers, cast out demons.
Freely you received, freely give.

MATTHEW 10:8

The generous man will be prosperous,
And he who waters will himself be watered.

PROVERBS 11:25

_God, let my life be a love song to You. Let it be so valuable to the work
of Your kingdom that should the need arise before my work is complete,
You will see fit to save me from trouble._

CONNECTED MEMBERS

One night I woke up needing to use the facilities. As I rounded the bed, I hit my toe and split it open! At that moment, a whole lot of other stuff started happening. The nerve in my toe talked to my ankle, which had a conversation with my leg, and my leg talked to my hip to say, "Get up off the ground." They worked in sync to communicate to my brain, which told the left leg, "You gotta carry this all by yourself." Then the brain sent a message to the mouth to let the neighborhood know how the toe felt. So everybody within the sound of my voice heard, "AHHHHHH!"

Just as all the members of my body are connected, so that messages can be sent and received very quickly, so we are designed for the body of Christ. The purpose of the church is not merely sermons and songs, but to be an environment of linkage: brother to brother, sister to sister, saint to saint, all to Christ! You are meant to be connected!

For even as the body is one and yet has many members,
and all the members of the body, though they are many,
are one body, so also is Christ.

I CORINTHIANS 12:12

For if anyone thinks he is something
when he is nothing, he deceives himself.

GALATIANS 6:3

day

64

For through the grace given to me
I say to everyone among you not to think
more highly of himself than he ought to think;
but to think so as to have sound judgment,
as God has allotted to each a measure of faith.

ROMANS 12:3

_Father God, thank You for choosing which part of the body I would be,
and for intending me for connection. Lead me in connecting
with the body of Christ, in love, for Your glory._

FORGIVE TO BE RELEASED

Forgiveness means to release a person from an obligation. It is the choice to release a person from a wrong committed against you. Forgiveness does not mean approving, excusing, justifying, or pretending not to be hurt. It's not repressing or pushing it in the basement of your mind so that you don't have to think about it. It's the decision to push the delete button after a wrong done against you.

The amazing thing about forgiveness is that it releases you, too. We have all seen a dog being held hostage by a leash. It can go a little distance, but once it goes too far, it gets yanked back or is simply unable to move forward. When the dog is collared, it stays stuck.

Forgiveness uncollars you from bitterness, anger, resentment, wrath, revenge, and all the links in a chain called unforgiveness.

So whether you need to forgive, or need to be forgiven, you can experience a supernatural release that leads to peace of mind and heart.

So, as those who have been chosen of God, holy and beloved,
put on a heart of compassion, kindness, humility, gentleness and patience;
bearing with one another, and forgiving each other, whoever has a complaint
against anyone; just as the Lord forgave you, so also should you.

COLOSSIANS 3:12–13

Be kind to one another, tender-hearted,
forgiving each other, just as God in Christ also has forgiven you.

EPHESIANS 4:32

In addition to all these things put on love,

which is the perfect bond of unity.

COLOSSIANS 3:14 NASB

day

65

Lord, place on my heart anyone I need to forgive.

And give me the boldness to apologize

when I have wronged another person.

A KIND WELCOME

In biblical times, they didn't have hotels on every corner. They didn't have places you could stop for a rest, grab a Starbucks, and do some laps in the pool with your key card entrance and scratchy towels to dry off with. So when you were a traveler going from place to place, you were absolutely dependent upon the hospitality of others. You needed others to open their hearts, their homes, their refrigerators, and their kindness to you. Because without them, days could be difficult, especially during times of persecution. Back then, hospitality wasn't just a word. It was something you depended on to make it.

The Greek word for *hospitality* means to fondly receive a guest; to kindly welcome a stranger. The reason God asks us to show hospitality is because it attacks our selfishness. Christian fellowship is more than a handshake, a pat on the back, and a "God bless you." It's about the meeting of needs and the showing of love in God's way.

Be hospitable to one another without complaint.

I PETER 4:9

A widow is to be put on the list only if ...
she has shown hospitality to strangers,
if she has washed the saints' feet,
if she has assisted those in distress,
and if she has devoted herself to every good work.

I TIMOTHY 5:9–10

**Share with the Lord's people
who are in need. Practice hospitality.**

ROMANS 12:13 NIV

_Father, it is not within my nature to welcome people warmly and without
restriction. But it is within Yours, so I surrender my selfishness to You
and ask for Your guidance in showing Your kind of hospitality._

SHINING FOR OTHERS

There's a major difference between headlights and streetlights. Headlights on a car show where it's going. They assist the driver in seeing the road. Streetlights, on the other hand, are for everyone who passes by. God not only wants to give you headlights; He wants you to become a streetlight so that others can see. If you are filled with the Spirit, your streetlight will make a difference everywhere you go.

Are you a sharing Christian? Not just on one occasion, but as a lifestyle? God doesn't share with you occasionally; He shares regularly, day in and day out. Sharing is a tangible, visible expression of gratitude to the Lord. It's not only a way that you can shine brightly for others, but it's a way that you can thank God every day for what He's done for you.

Little children,
let us not love with word or with tongue,
but in deed and truth.

I JOHN 3:18

And they exceeded our expectations:
They gave themselves first of all to the Lord,
and then by the will of God also to us.

II CORINTHIANS 8:5 NIV

day

67

Give, and it will be given to you.
They will pour into your lap a good measure—
pressed down, shaken together, and running over.
For by your standard of measure
it will be measured to you in return.

LUKE 6:38

_____
_____
_____
_____
_____
_____
_____
_____
_____
_____
_____
_____
_____
_____
_____

Father, may I be the type of Christian who lives in daily gratitude.
May my willingness to share be a light for all to see and live by.

PEACE NOT WAR

Alfred Nobel was the Swedish physicist who invented dynamite. His intentions were to create an explosive that would help move rock away so people could build roads and buildings. He wanted to create a powerful force that would make life better.

A problem came when people took his creation and started to use it for destructive purposes. People started using dynamite to kill other people and to make war. It saddened Dr. Nobel so much that he took nine million dollars and put it in an account, then started rewarding people who were promoting peace. We know that as the Nobel Peace Prize, of course. It came about because what he had intended was being used incorrectly, and he wanted to award those who were following his intentions.

God is looking for people who are making peace so that He can reward them and honor them by His name. It takes courage to stand out for peace. Are you up for the challenge?

Depart from evil and do good;
Seek peace and pursue it.

PSALM 34:14

Pursue peace with all men, and the sanctification
without which no one will see the Lord.

HEBREWS 12:14

If possible,
so far as it depends on you,
be at peace with all men.

ROMANS 12:18

God, it's one thing to simply not participate

in the evil intentions of others.

It's another to actively pursue the opposite.

Make me an instrument of Your peace.

SURRENDERED BLESSINGS

The term *spiritual bankruptcy* sounds negative. But in truth, it's the way to be blessed. While it's possible to have stuff and be blessed, it's also possible to have stuff and not be blessed. The only way to blessing God's way is through complete surrender to Him.

When you confess to heaven that you're unable to fix yourself, it opens the way for heaven to come to your aid. When you mourn over your own sin, then God can comfort you with His forgiveness. When you are meek and gentle, then God can trust you with His inheritance. That way, when God does satisfy you, you will be willing to go and satisfy someone else.

When you show others mercy, then God will be merciful back to you. When you protect your heart and keep it undivided, then you will see God intervene in your circumstances. You will see God for yourself. You won't piggyback onto someone else's testimony; you will be blessed on earth *and* through your inheritance in heaven.

Blessed are the poor in spirit,
for theirs is the kingdom of heaven.

MATTHEW 5:3

For the sorrow that is according to the will of God
produces a repentance without regret, leading to salvation,
but the sorrow of the world produces death.

II CORINTHIANS 7:10

The sacrifices of God are a broken spirit;
A broken and a contrite heart,
O God, You will not despise.

PSALM 51:17

Lord, world culture would say that more is better and pride is a right.
But kingdom culture celebrates the poor spirit in surrender to You.
I give You my heart and ask You to make me more and more like You.

SHIPS VS. SUBMARINES

Each person gets to decide whether they're a ship or a submarine. Ships sit on the water, and as long as the waters are calm, the ship is calm. But when things get choppy, the ship will toss around at the mercy of Mother Nature. Because happiness is based on what happens.

A submarine can come to the surface, too. Happiness happens to a submarine person. But a submarine is not limited to the surface. No matter how intense the weather, it can only affect the water down 25 feet. And a submarine can go 26 feet down. Or 126 or 526 feet down! The reason a submarine doesn't worry about chaos on the surface is because it doesn't live on the surface. It belongs down deep.

God doesn't want you to be a ship, bounced around and tossed by the waves. He wants you to be a submarine, so that when things get rough externally, you can say, "Okay, I'm going down deep. Because I have something deep inside that doesn't depend on what's happening on the outside."

Which are you, a ship or a submarine? Are you building a deep and lasting understanding of God's heart? Or are you more prone to being tossed about?

Let your roots grow down into Him, and let your lives be built on Him.
Then your faith will grow strong in the truth you were taught,
and you will overflow with thankfulness.

COLOSSIANS 2:7 NLT

I am the vine, you are the branches;
he who abides in Me and I in him, he bears much fruit,
for apart from Me you can do nothing.

JOHN 15:5

And you who are left in Judah,

who have escaped the ravages of the siege,

will put roots down in your own soil

and grow up and flourish.

ISAIAH 37:31 NLT

Lord, thank You for Your law of liberty,

which gives me a place to run no matter the situation.

May I continue to dig deeper into Your safety and wisdom.

THE FRUIT OF ABIDING

Love is not an abstract concept. It's a real deal, boots-on-the-ground sort of behavior. In fact, do you know what the Bible says about how we'll know love? We know it by this: that Jesus Christ laid His life down for us. Love is beyond sacrificial. It is both the motivation and the goal of the Christian life.

Because Jesus laid down His life as a demonstration of love, we know that love is a demonstration and not just an articulation. You can't just talk your way through loving somebody, nor can you act based on whatever emotion you feel for that person. God puts people in your path who need to be seen, empathized with, and then helped. If you are abiding in His love and willing to keep your heart open to His leading, then love will be the fruit of Your relationship with God.

Think of a time when someone sacrificially demonstrated love for you. What effect did it have on your situation? On your attitude? On your choices from that moment forward?

We know love by this, that He laid down His life for us;
and we ought to lay down our lives for the brethren.

I JOHN 3:16

There is no fear in love; but perfect love casts out fear,
because fear involves punishment,
and the one who fears is not perfected in love.

I JOHN 4:18

And whoever in the name of a disciple
gives to one of these little ones even
a cup of cold water to drink, truly I say to you,
he shall not lose his reward.

MATTHEW 10:42

_____

_____

_____

_____

_____

_____

_____

_____

_____

_____

_____

_____

_____

_____

_____

_____

_____

Jesus, thank You for your incredible, unmatchable,
amazing demonstration of love. I will forever be seeking
to love You and love others, as You have loved me.

TOUCHED BY THE SON

In the spring and summer, it gets hotter. And as it gets hotter, it usually becomes evident when you've spent a lot of time in the sun. You're going to be fanning yourself, sweating, and your skin might burn a bit. In other words, it will become evident that the sun has affected you. Many will wish not to be affected for any extended amount of time by the sun, so they're going to get out of it as quickly as possible because they want to be cool.

As a Christian, it will become evident when the Son has affected you. And the way it will become evident is through the ways that you touch the people around you. No matter how many church services you attend, no matter how much praise you offer, no matter how much hand waving or pew flipping you're involved in—if lives are not benefited by the time you are spending in the Son, then He hasn't quite rubbed off on you.

The longer you're in the Son, the more sensitive you are to others. And Jesus wants you to know that the way you tangibly know you love Him is that you're touching others.

As each one has received a special gift,
employ it in serving one another as good stewards
of the manifold grace of God.

I PETER 4:10

Therefore if anyone is in Christ, he is a new creature;
the old things passed away; behold, new things have come.

II CORINTHIANS 5:17

We know love by this,

that He laid down His life for us;

and we ought to lay down

our lives for the brethren.

I JOHN 3:16

Jesus, I want to be close enough to You, and spend so much time with You,

that I can't help but affect the lives of the people around me.

Thank You for Your light and life.

UNWANTED GIFTS

Did you ever have somebody buy you something for your birthday that you did not want, did not ask for, and could not use? It became a wasted gift. You put it in the attic, threw it in the trash, or worse yet, you gave it to somebody else on their birthday!

Unfortunately, people give Jesus a lot of stuff that He can't use. They give Him something He doesn't want because they feel they need to do something. What Jesus says He wants is for you to touch the life of another in His name. He wants you to touch the life of somebody who can't help you back. They're the naked ones—without clothes, without food, without resources. They're thirsty. They're in prison. They can't do anything for you.

We live in a world full of business deals. There's nothing wrong with business. But life with Jesus is not a business relationship. More than your time or talent, He wants your heart. Ask Him to lead you to a life in need of a holy touch today.

One who is gracious to a poor man lends to the LORD,
And He will repay him for his good deed.

PROVERBS 19:17

And if you give yourself to the hungry
And satisfy the desire of the afflicted,
Then your light will rise in darkness
And your gloom will become like midday.

ISAIAH 58:10

day

73

**Pure and undefiled religion
in the sight of our God and Father is this:
to visit orphans and widows in their distress,
and to keep oneself unstained by the world.**

JAMES 1:27

_____
_____
_____
_____
_____
_____
_____
_____
_____
_____
_____
_____
_____
_____
_____
_____

Father, may I never again give You a gift that You can't use.
Thank You for Your mercy as I learn to love as You love.

INTERNAL BLESSINGS

God blesses us with an inner peace and joy—an overall inner well-being that gives us the sustenance we need to help people. A lot of folks think blessing comes on the outside, with stuff and success. Happiness can come from the external. But the problem with happiness is that it depends on what happens. It is circumstantial.

When God talks about blessing, He means building a playground in your heart.

We've all taken our kids to fast-food restaurants. The kids' meal comes with chicken or a burger, and the kids will eat and drink. But for most of us, we would lean toward one of those places that has a play area. When we took our kids, they would skip the eating and drinking and run straight to the playground. Sometimes we had to make them come from the playground to eat because while the eating and drinking was appreciated, it was not the priority for them.

God says that when it comes to being blessed, don't be satisfied with the stuff outside that you put inside, the eating and drinking. Make sure that you have a playground in your soul.

For the kingdom of God is not eating and drinking,
but righteousness and peace and joy in the Holy Spirit.

ROMANS 14:17

Though you have not seen Him, you love Him,
and though you do not see Him now, but believe in Him,
you greatly rejoice with joy inexpressible and full of glory.

I PETER 1:8

Go then, eat your bread in happiness
and drink your wine with a cheerful heart;
for God has already approved your works.

ECCLESIASTES 9:7

_____

_____

_____

_____

_____

_____

_____

_____

_____

_____

_____

_____

_____

_____

_____

_____

_____

_____

*Lord, together I believe You and I can build a wonderful playground
of joy in my soul. Forgive me for times when I have looked
for happiness externally. Help me to look within from now on.*

THE LEAST OF THESE

When you go to the doctor, it's usually to fix something you don't see. It's something that's on the inside that takes you to the doctor, generally speaking, because the part that you don't see is critical.

Every member in the body of Christ must be viewed as valuable. Not every member has the same level of responsibility. Not every member has the same job description—but every job matters. There are no big "I"s and little "you"s in the family of God.

When you go to church, the floor has been vacuumed, the pews have been polished, the bathrooms have been stocked. You may not notice. But you sure would if the floors were dirty, the pews were cluttered, and the bathrooms were out of toilet paper!

You should never look down on a person because they're behind the scenes. It's the invisible parts that make the visible parts work. How you treat the folk who don't have the name or notoriety, the money or fancy car, the "least of these" reflects on how you treat God. Every member of His body matters.

*Whoever in the name of a disciple gives
to one of these little ones even a cup of cold water to drink,
truly I say to you, he shall not lose his reward.*

MATTHEW 10:42

*Then He will answer them, "Truly I say to you,
to the extent that you did not do it to one of the least of these,
you did not do it to Me."*

MATTHEW 25:45

Whoever then humbles himself as this child,
he is the greatest in the kingdom of heaven.

MATTHEW 18:4

Lord, give me the eyes to see people the way You do.
Help me to treat all equally and to notice the unseen.

TWO KINDS OF FORGIVENESS

Unilateral forgiveness is to forgive those who haven't asked for it. On the cross, Jesus said, "Father, forgive them; for they do not know what they are doing" (Luke 23:34). It could be forgiving someone who has died, someone you can't find, or someone with whom you have no communication. It could be forgiving someone who simply hasn't asked for it.

Transactional forgiveness comes because a person has confessed and repented of a wrong done against you. It goes two ways. They've said the words, followed them with action, and made room for reconciliation. Reconciliation is almost impossible in unilateral forgiveness, but when there are two willing parties, reconciliation can be beautiful.

Jesus paid for the sins of the whole world; that was unilateral. But what He offers is transactional. Because if you come to Christ in faith, you will be reconciled with the Father. Jesus' sacrifice reconciled the Father with you. Accepting Christ will reconcile you with the Father.

Both kinds of forgiveness release debt. But transactional forgiveness allows for reconciliation.

But Jesus was saying, "Father, forgive them;
for they do not know what they are doing."

LUKE 23:34

So watch yourselves.
"If your brother or sister sins against you, rebuke them;
and if they repent, forgive them."

LUKE 17:3 NIV

For God was pleased to have all His fullness
dwell in Him, and through Him
to reconcile to Himself all things,
whether things on earth or things in heaven,
by making peace through His blood,
shed on the cross.

COLOSSIANS 1:19–20 NIV

day

76

*Father, give me the courage to forgive those
I can't confront or communicate with.
And when necessary, give me the wisdom
to have conversations that lead to reconciliation.*

BIBLICAL HOSPITALITY

One day, a gentleman knocked on the door of an apartment, and a lady opened it. She said, "Can I help you?"

He said, "One of your neighbors doesn't have enough rent. They only have a couple days left before they'll get kicked out. I'm going around and simply asking if anyone would like to help this family by paying this month's rent."

The lady said, "Oh yes, I wouldn't want to see one of my neighbors kicked out! Let me get something." As she gave the money to the gentleman at the door, she asked, "By the way, who are you?"

He replied, "The landlord."

It's easy, when we're going to benefit, to look like we're hospitable. But the biblical doctrine of hospitality—that is, welcoming in an authentic way—has to do with serving even those who can do nothing for you in return. When you serve people who can only do things for you in return, that's called a business deal. A win-win. But when you do something with nothing expected in return, and you do it with the right attitude, that's biblical hospitality. That's welcoming authentically. And THAT is what the Bible says Christians ought to be about.

For I was hungry, and you gave Me something to eat;
I was thirsty, and you gave Me something to drink;
I was a stranger, and you invited Me in.

MATTHEW 25:35

The King will answer and say to them,
"Truly I say to you, to the extent that you did it to one of
these brothers of Mine, even the least of them, you did it to Me."

MATTHEW 25:40

Do not neglect to show hospitality
to strangers, for by this some have
entertained angels without knowing it.

HEBREWS 13:2

God, You call us to a more surrendered,
more loving version of who we think we are, and for that I am grateful.
Teach me to welcome others as though they were You I was serving.

INVEST WISELY

Growing up, my favorite game was Monopoly. I am an entrepreneur by nature, and of course, my goal in the game was to acquire Boardwalk and Park Place as quickly as possible. I'd build green houses and red hotels on those properties as fast as I could, and I'd just take over that neighborhood. If you came around my side of the board, watch out! Monopoly is not about sharing; it's about accumulating all you can and sharing nothing. But when the paper money is put away and the box lid is closed, the game is over.

When we become a caring, sharing church in God's power and grace, all needs will be met. It's been said that if every Christian in America took God seriously and gave generously, then every social need of every Christian in the nation would be taken care of.

No one has ever seen a hearse towing a U-Haul because you can't take it with you. Investing on earth lasts for a short while. But investing in the kingdom lasts forever.

So, when the box lid closes on your life, what will people know of your generosity? Whom will you have shared with, and how will lives have been impacted? Right now, you can make a huge difference.

It is well with the man who is gracious and lends;
He will maintain his cause in judgment.

PSALM 112:5

And God is able to make all grace abound to you,
so that always having all sufficiency in everything,
you may have an abundance for every good deed;
as it is written, "HE SCATTERED ABROAD, HE GAVE TO THE POOR,
HIS RIGHTEOUSNESS ENDURES FOREVER."

II CORINTHIANS 9:8-9

Now this I say, he who sows sparingly
will also reap sparingly,
and he who sows bountifully
will also reap bountifully

II CORINTHIANS 9:6

Lord, search my heart for selfishness and burn it all away.
I want to be a cheerful, generous giver.

BLESSED ARE THE MEEK

Meekness is power under control. There was once an advertisement for a certain brand of soup. It featured a famous NFL player being tough on the field. But when his mom told him to come in and eat his soup, he went right away. The tough, strong player was exercising control over his power, by listening to his mom.

Meekness has to do with yielding to the legitimate authority in your life. It is a willingness to bow. The biggest players on a football team are the offensive linemen. They're usually the biggest and strongest, but they're also the ones who get the lowest when it's time to run a play. Going low is where they get their leverage to be the most effective.

Some people have a very hard time submitting to the spiritual authority in their lives. And once you have that rebellious spirit, you cancel the work of God, walking you through whatever it is that you need His power to overcome. But meekness, when activated, gives God room to work. When you bow to Him, He can become bigger and do more, both in and through you.

So get rid of all the filth and evil in your lives,
and humbly accept the word God has planted in your hearts,
for it has the power to save your souls.

JAMES 1:21 NLT

Let it be the hidden person of the heart,
with the imperishable quality of a gentle and quiet spirit,
which is precious in the sight of God.

I PETER 3:4

But the humble will inherit the land
And will delight themselves
in abundant prosperity.

PSALM 37:11

Father, Jesus was the picture of meekness
when He humbled Himself as a baby and became like us.
Give me a heart to submit fully to Your authority and trust You to lead.

INVERTER FAITH

When we went to visit my parents in Baltimore, we noticed that their microwave was broken. My children decided to go and buy their grandparents a new one. The microwave they bought was new technology at the time, called an inverter. Most of us have a microwave that heats food from the outside in. It's possible for the food to appear cooked, but you'll discover that it's hot on the outside and gets colder and colder as you go in. With an inverter, it heats food from the inside out.

Some people have a microwave faith, where they appear on fire for God on the outside, but their soul is cold. With an inverter faith, if a person is hot for God on the outside, you know they're smokin' on the inside! They've worked out their faith from the inside out.

God is not against a hot outside. He's not against you looking blessed and on fire. I love seeing people fully blessed with all that He can give them externally—but not at the expense of the soul. God wants your inside to fuel your outside, instead of banking on your hot outside to make the inside better.

Beloved, I pray that in all respects you may prosper
and be in good health, just as your soul prospers.

III JOHN 1:2

Now may the God of hope fill you with all joy and peace in believing,
so that you will abound in hope by the power of the Holy Spirit.

ROMANS 15:13

For You have been my help,

And in the shadow of Your wings

I sing for joy.

PSALM 63:7

_____

_____

_____

_____

_____

_____

_____

_____

_____

_____

_____

_____

_____

_____

_____

_____

_____

_____

Father, may my outside reflect my inside
and not the other way around.

KNOWN FOR LOVE

Everyone has a birthmark of some sort. It might be your fingerprints, a different-colored part of skin, a certain wrinkle, or placement of hair that makes you totally unique and identifies you to others. When you are adopted into God's family, you receive His birthmark as well. That birthmark is love (John 13:35). God's definition of love marks us out as unique.

God's definition of love makes a distinction between *love* and *like*. *Like* has to do with some emotional detachment. When you like someone, you're comfortable with them. You enjoy them, and there's something about them that makes you feel connected.

Love, on the other hand, is the decision you make to compassionately and righteously seek the well-being of another, whether you like them or not. In other words, biblical love does not require an emotional attachment. Of course it's great to like the person you love. But the Bible tells us to love even our enemies. The big difference between *like* and *love* is that *like* is an emotion and *love* is a decision.

Whom in your life do you love without liking? Whom do you love *and* like?

By this all men will know that you are My disciples,
if you have love for one another.

JOHN 13:35

Above all, keep fervent in your love for one another,
because love covers a multitude of sins.

I PETER 4:8

Love is patient, love is kind and is not jealous;

love does not brag and is not arrogant,

does not act unbecomingly;

it does not seek its own, is not provoked,

does not take into account a wrong suffered.

I CORINTHIANS 13:4–5

_____
_____
_____
_____
_____
_____
_____
_____
_____
_____
_____
_____
_____
_____
_____
_____

God, You are the perfect example of loving well.
Give me the courage and maturity to love those I don't like,
and even to learn to like those whom I am loving.

LOVE GIVES SOMETHING UP

Love is an issue of action, not merely an issue of words. A single woman gets approached by a single guy, and that guy has all the right things to say. He tells her she's beautiful, and that he loves her. But he doesn't do anything to demonstrate his love. She might as well tell the man to find another pastime. It's nice to have your ears tickled, and you can appreciate kind words, but if he's not showing his love for you, then it's not what God calls love. It might be some other word: In the case of romance, maybe it's "like" on steroids! But love has to be demonstrated in order to be declared real.

Biblical love is demonstrable, and it's demonstrable by sacrifice. It means giving something up for another person. Because "God so loved the world, that He gave" (John 3:16, emphasis added), and He expects the same of us.

Consider your current relationships and what you sacrifice on their behalf. It could be time, or comfort, or even using words when words don't come easy for you. Ask God to show you what true love is.

"Which of these three do you think proved
to be a neighbor to the man who fell into the robbers' hands?"
And he said, "The one who showed mercy toward him."
Then Jesus said to him, "Go and do the same."
LUKE 10:36−37

Let all that you do be done in love.
I CORINTHIANS 16:14

For God so loved the world,
that He gave His only begotten Son,
that whoever believes in Him shall not perish,
but have eternal life.

JOHN 3:16

_____

_____

_____

_____

_____

_____

_____

_____

_____

_____

_____

_____

_____

_____

_____

_____

_____

_____

_____

_____

_____

Lord, let my love be demonstrated in ways that show You to others.
Give me courage and strength to love sacrificially.

THE AROMA OF CHRIST

One day, a man was in line behind another man at the store. And he said, "Excuse me, sir, but you smell like roses."

The second man said, "Yes, I'm a florist. I stand in the flower shop all day, so I smell like where I hang out."

What about you? Where do you hang out, spiritually? With whom do you hang out? When folks take a sniff of you, what are they going to smell? Because if you've been in the presence of God, that aroma is going to rub off on you. Do you remember that song "I'm just a love machine"? Old school, I know! But the point is, when you're in the presence of God on a regular basis, then His love is going to crank out of you like it was always meant to.

Second Corinthians 2:15 calls us the fragrance of Christ to folks when we spend time around Him. Are you spending enough time with Him to let Him rub off on you?

For we are a fragrance of Christ to God among those
who are being saved and among those who are perishing.

II CORINTHIANS 2:15

Walk in love, just as Christ also loved you
and gave Himself up for us,
an offering and a sacrifice
to God as a fragrant aroma.

EPHESIANS 5:2

**Follow God's example, therefore,
as dearly loved children
and walk in the way of love.**

EPHESIANS 5:1–2 NIV

*God, thank You for inviting me so close to You
that I can actually give off Your fragrance.
May I be a pleasing aroma to You.*

THE LEAST OF THESE

In Matthew 25:42–43, Jesus talks about what it means to serve others. He says that when we do good works for others, we are doing good works for Him, too. And when we ignore the good works that He prepared in advance for us to do, we are passing up the chance to do good works for God.

When Jesus sits on His glorious throne at the end of time, that's when He hands out His rewards. He says that when you help others, you are representing His name.

In America, we have inconveniences and minor sufferings but not the kinds that Christians around the world have. Our lives are not at stake on a daily basis. So when we set aside our discomfort and reach out to help another, we are choosing the kingdom.

Do nothing from selfishness or empty conceit,
but with humility of mind regard one another
as more important than yourselves.

PHILIPPIANS 2:3

Then they themselves also will answer,
"Lord, when did we see You hungry, or thirsty, or a stranger,
or naked, or sick, or in prison, and did not take care of You?"
Then He will answer them, "Truly I say to you, to the extent
that you did not do it to one of the least of these,
you did not do it to Me."

MATTHEW 25:44–45

**Do not merely look out
for your own personal interests,
but also for the interests of others.**

PHILIPPIANS 2:4

_____
_____
_____
_____
_____
_____
_____
_____
_____
_____
_____
_____
_____
_____
_____
_____
_____
_____
_____
_____
_____
_____

*God, it will take the unblinding of my eyes and
the unveiling of my heart to see those who need a hand in Your name.
Walk with me as I seek to serve.*

SERVING OTHERS

Before a wedding, a bride is typically surrounded by other ladies who are designated to make sure that everything is just right. Bridesmaids, coordinators, mothers, sisters, and friends make sure that the veil, dress, and makeup are just right. Because when the bride walks down the aisle, she is meant to walk in radiating her full glory for her groom.

Servanthood is the willingness to humble oneself and act for the benefit of another in the name of Christ. It is an attitude, followed by an action, that wants to facilitate the improvement of the condition of another. You become a servant when you're able to come alongside someone, to assist them in some way that will improve them spiritually or circumstantially. You want to better the situation however you can.

What makes Jesus look really good are the people who come alongside Him to serve others. And if you have accepted Him as your personal sin bearer, then you've been called to serve.

For by grace you have been saved through faith;
and that not of yourselves, it is the gift of God;
not as a result of works, so that no one may boast.
For we are His workmanship, created in Christ Jesus for good works,
which God prepared beforehand so that we would walk in them.

EPHESIANS 2:8–10

The greatest among you shall be your servant.

MATTHEW 23:11

day

85

God is not unjust;
He will not forget your work and
the love you have shown Him
as you have helped His people
and continue to help them.

HEBREWS 6:10 NIV

_____
_____
_____
_____
_____
_____
_____
_____
_____
_____
_____
_____
_____
_____

*God, help me to humble myself and
assist others in ways that will bring glory to Your name.*

RANSOMED

One day before school, a boy brought his mother a list. It was a bill for services rendered. "For mowing the lawn, $2. For emptying the trash, $2. For cleaning my room, $2. For doing the dishes this week, $2. Mama, you owe me $8."

When he got home from school, the boy received eight dollars and a list from his mom: "For carrying you nine months, with nausea, $O. For cooking three meals a day for 15 years, $O. For working overtime to buy you those sneakers, $O. For losing sleep and wages when you broke your leg, $O. Son, you owe me nothing." The boy recognized the price his mother had paid, and he gave back the money, because he was responding to the goodness of his mother.

We've gotten so used to Jesus. We've forgotten that He laid down His life for us at no charge, purely out of love and a desire for us to be in relationship with God. We've forgotten how freely He offers Himself to us, even when we don't do the same thing in return. We've forgotten what a good God He is.

When you really recognize God's goodness, you want to serve Him. Serving God becomes a passion, an opportunity, and a privilege.

It was for freedom that Christ set us free.

GALATIANS 5:1

For there is one God, and one mediator also between God and men,
the man Christ Jesus, who gave Himself as a ransom for all,
the testimony given at the proper time.

I TIMOTHY 2:5-6

The wages of sin is death,
but the free gift of God is eternal life
in Christ Jesus our Lord.

ROMANS 6:23

Lord God, I have gotten used to You and
forgotten what You paid on my behalf.
Make me aware again so that I can serve You with joy and passion.

MOVING IN
THE SAME DIRECTION

Unity is uniqueness moving in a common direction. An orchestra is unified, not because all the instruments are the same, but because the different instruments are playing the same song. A football team isn't unified because all the positions are the same, but because all the different positions are working together toward a common goal line. Unity recognizes and welcomes uniqueness, as long as the goal of the uniqueness is one purpose.

You and I are not trying to make each other resemble one another. You and I are to recognize and embrace differences, as long as those differences are moving in concert toward a common end. Satan wants to break up unity because he wants to keep God out of the equation. So when we choose unity, we are choosing God's design, God's plan, and God's purpose.

May the God who gives perseverance and encouragement grant you
to be of the same mind with one another according to Christ Jesus,
so that with one accord you may with one voice glorify
the God and Father of our Lord Jesus Christ.

ROMANS 15:5–6

Now I urge you, brethren, keep your eye on those who cause dissensions
and hindrances contrary to the teaching which you learned,
and turn away from them.

ROMANS 16:17

I exhort you, brethren, by the name of our Lord Jesus Christ, that you all agree and that there be no divisions among you, but that you be made complete in the same mind and in the same judgment.

I CORINTHIANS 1:10

_____
_____
_____
_____
_____
_____
_____
_____
_____
_____
_____
_____
_____
_____
_____
_____

Father, unify us as the Trinity is unified, separate and unique but common in essence and purpose.

JUSTICE AND MERCY

The Hebrew word for *kindness* in the Bible is *hesed*, which has to do with the compassion of God. God's got two sides to Him—one of justice and one of compassion. While He demands respect and fear of His authority, He balances it with mercy.

When parents are all about justice, they demand obedience to the rules. Rules and obedience are legitimate, as long as kids know their parents care about them, too. There will be consequences for actions, both good and bad— but there will be hugs, love, and acceptance as a person. Compassion and kindness are what train a child to choose well in the future.

Do you tend to lean more toward following rules or toward mercy? Rules without compassion can feel cruel and religious. Compassion without rules can feel lawless and disrespectful. On the tightrope of life, we are meant to live with God's way of balancing both.

What does the LORD require of you
But to do justice, to love kindness,
And to walk humbly with your God?

MICAH 6:8

Be merciful, just as your Father is merciful.

LUKE 6:36

I forgave you all that debt because you pleaded
with me. Should you not also have had mercy . . .
in the same way that I had mercy on you?

MATTHEW 18:32–33

_____
_____
_____
_____
_____
_____
_____
_____
_____
_____
_____
_____
_____
_____
_____
_____
_____

God, in my dealings with people,
guide me in having the perfect balance of respect for rules
and merciful compassion.

YOUR ALLOTTED PORTION

Back in biblical times, God had a Promised Land laid out for the nation of Israel as an inheritance. The journey required obedience and trust—following a pillar of cloud by day and a pillar of fire by night and listening to Moses' leadership. God said to Israel, *If you are willing to submit to your legitimate authority, I will take you to this land and give you your allotted portion.*

Unfortunately, Israel allowed themselves to be swayed by pride and fear. They didn't trust God and submit to authority. So the first generation never reached the Promised Land. The absence of meekness cut them off from the land.

God says in Ephesians 1 that everything He's ever going to do for you, He's already done. What you haven't seen accomplished in your life yet is simply because your allotted portion will happen over your lifetime. He has determined the right increments.

In order to receive your portion, walk humbly with God and trust His process. When you do, He will pour out His blessings.

For those blessed by Him will inherit the land,
But those cursed by Him will be cut off.

PSALM 37:22

Blessed be the God and Father of our Lord Jesus Christ,
who has blessed us with every spiritual blessing
in the heavenly places in Christ,

EPHESIANS 1:3

day
89

Wait for the LORD and keep His way,
And He will exalt you to inherit the land;
When the wicked are cut off, you will see it.

PSALM 37:34

Father, thank You for blessing us with every blessing.
Lead me to walk humbly with You.

THE RIGHT BANK

If your bank account is with Bank of America, but you go writing withdrawal slips at Wells Fargo or Citigroup or Chase, you won't get a cent. Because that's not where your stuff is. A withdrawal slip isn't enough to withdraw money from a bank if you don't have anything saved up there.

Ephesians 1:3 says that your blessings are "in the heavenly places." You can't withdraw your allotment from God if you are not under His legitimate authority—the Bank of the Heavenly Realms. You can't have a better marriage, a better career, stronger relationships, or any other good thing apart from God. You can do some things independently of Him, but you can't have the well-being or the lasting effects if you are not withdrawing from where your true blessings are stored. But with God, every allotted thing that God has declared for you is in the heavenly realms, and it will come to you.

In what areas are you trying to operate while out from under God's covering? In what ways have you seen God pour out blessing due to your willingness to let Him lead? How has God's authority affected your relationships and ventures?

I am the vine, you are the branches;
he who abides in Me and I in him, he bears much fruit,
for apart from Me you can do nothing.

JOHN 15:5

Do not be afraid, little flock, for your Father
has chosen gladly to give you the kingdom.

LUKE 12:32

But let all who take refuge in You be glad,

Let them ever sing for joy;

And may You shelter them,

That those who love Your name may exult in You.

PSALM 5:11

Lord, I can't begin to comprehend the blessings

You have laid out and allotted for me.

May I live in the knowledge and faith of Your abundant blessings.

ACTS OF KINDNESS

In a cruel world, we need more kindness (am I right?). But what can we do to make a real difference? Sometimes it seems that our efforts don't matter—that our actions and words, no matter how kind they are, don't have a chance of lighting up the darkness. But the truth is, even what we see as our smallest acts of kindness can make a huge difference in the way our world functions. Think about it—what if all Christians cultivated a heart of kindness in their everyday lives? What if kindness became so ingrained in our souls, that it instantly poured out of us in every situation and every interaction throughout every day of our lives? Now, that would make an impact—a kingdom impact.

What are acts of kindness? Acts of kindness can be anything from offering to carry groceries for someone who is struggling (maybe an elderly person or a young mom), or bringing a cup of coffee to a co-worker, or helping a neighbor, taking someone lunch, tipping more than standard, offering to help someone who looks lost, holding the door open, letting someone in line ahead of you, to simply being intentional about what you say and seeking to encourage someone who is down.

What acts of kindness do you plan to accomplish today?

How can you make this a part of your everyday life?

But love your enemies, and do good, and lend, expecting nothing in return; and your reward will be great, and you will be sons of the Most High; for He Himself is kind to ungrateful and evil men.

LUKE 6:35

So, as those who have been chosen of God, holy and beloved, put on a heart of compassion, kindness, humility, gentleness and patience; bearing with one another, and forgiving each other, whoever has a complaint against anyone; just as the Lord forgave you, so also should you.

COLOSSIANS 3:12–13

She opens her mouth in wisdom,
And the teaching of kindness is on her tongue.

PROVERBS 31:26

Lord, open my eyes to who may need Your kindness today and every day.
I want Your heart to be on full display in everything I do
and everywhere I go.

MEETING OTHERS' NEEDS

Imagine you knock on my door one day and tell me, "I'm really hungry. Can you help?" I see your need, I feel your need, and I have some food. Now imagine that I begin exercising my knowledge of Scripture, and pontificate the great truths of the faith about God's ability to meet needs. I quote Philippians 4:19 to you: "My God will supply all your needs according to His riches in glory in Christ Jesus." I quote to you Philippians 3 and Psalm 37:25. I give you the Word of God, and even pronounce a blessing over you. Everything I said was right and also useless. You didn't need a sermon—you needed a sandwich!

When you have the capacity to meet a need, and yet you close your heart to the person and the situation, then God is the One who has been shut out from you. God *wants* to be with us, and He wants to meet your needs. That's why He keeps putting people in your path whose needs you are able to meet. But He won't force the issue. You get to choose whether or not you open your heart to love.

Pure and undefiled religion in the sight of our God and Father is this:
to visit orphans and widows in their distress,
and to keep oneself unstained by the world.

JAMES 1:27

If a brother or sister is without clothing and
in need of daily food, and one of you says to them,
"Go in peace, be warmed and be filled," yet you do not give them
what is necessary for their body, what use is that?

JAMES 2:15–16

**By this all people will know
that you are My disciples:
if you have love for one another.**

JOHN 13:35 NASB

_____
_____
_____
_____
_____
_____
_____
_____
_____
_____
_____
_____
_____
_____
_____
_____
_____
_____
_____

*Lord, help me to understand when more than words are necessary.
I ask for supernatural generosity and a heart to love like You.*

WELCOME HOME

Henry Morrison had been a missionary to Africa. He was on his way back home to the United States to retire. On his ship was the president of the United States. When the boat reached the harbor, there were throngs of people waiting to welcome the president. There were hundreds of people, a marching band, streamers, the whole nine yards.

One of the last people off of the ship was Henry. And he cried because no one was there to greet him and welcome him home. No one there to celebrate the years and years that he had spent serving the Lord.

Just then the Holy Spirit hit him with an epiphany. In his mind's eye, he saw himself in heaven one day. Henry saw thousands and thousands of people there to greet him home. There were people whose lives he had touched and even more people whose lives were touched by the lives he had touched. People cheered and chanted his name. And as he stood there on the ship's gangplank, he heard the Lord say to his spirit, *Henry, you're not home yet.*

Are you one who tends to want the world's approval and applause now? Or are you content to wait for your actual homecoming?

His master replied, "Well done, good and faithful servant!
You have been faithful with a few things; I will put you in charge
of many things. Come and share your master's happiness!"

MATTHEW 25:23 NIV

Therefore, prepare your minds for action, keep sober in spirit,
fix your hope completely on the grace to be brought to you
at the revelation of Jesus Christ.

I PETER 1:13

The LORD looks down from heaven
on the human race to see
if there is one who is wise,
one who seeks God.

PSALM 14:2 CSB

Lord, give me the courage to seek Your reward and Yours alone.
Help me to celebrate with those who are recognized now,
and rejoice in my hiddenness.

A CHALLENGE
AND A PURPOSE

John chapter 9 introduces us to a man who was born blind. At that time, people would ask what the parents had done wrong in order to have a special-needs child born to them. But Jesus had a different answer. He said, "It was neither *that* this man sinned, nor his parents; but *it* was so that the works of God might be displayed in him" (verse 3). Did you follow that? Jesus said, "The man is blind because I have a plan for him." Jesus sees the blind man's lack of sight not as a setback, but as a unique and captivating fulfillment of God's purposes.

The next time you run across somebody who faces different challenges from you, check on whether there's a message coming your way. Because God says the blind man was there for a divine reason and divine purpose.

Do you know someone who faces daily physical, tangible challenges? Ask God to direct your focus toward their purpose and quality of life.

Jesus answered, "It was neither *that* this man sinned, nor his parents; *but* it *was* so that the works of God might be displayed in him."

JOHN 9:3

"For I know the plans that I have for you," declares the LORD, *"plans for welfare and not for calamity to give you a future and a hope."*

JEREMIAH 29:11

We must work the works of Him
who sent Me as long as it is day;
night is coming when no one can work.
While I am in the world,
I am the Light of the world.

JOHN 9:4–5

Father, I confess that I tend to evaluate people by what I see.
Show me their special purposes,
and give me the ability to speak into their lives.

DENTED SOULS

Several years ago, a man ran into my car with his vehicle. Come to find out he was uninsured. So for a while, I had a dent in my car caused by somebody else who was unable to fix the problem. Then I had the dent fixed. I could have chosen to drive around with a dent in my car, caused by somebody else, being mad every day that they didn't fix it. Every time I went out to see that dent, I would've thought, *That no-good driver messed up my car.*

Unfortunately, a lot of folks are living with dents in their souls. Someone ran into their lives and put a dent there, and they spend so much time being mad that the person couldn't fix what they dented. With forgiveness, the dented soul could be repaired. But sometimes anger, vengefulness, and bitterness can become very comfortable to a person. They can forget how to live without those things, because every time they remember that dent, it justifies the anger.

Forgiveness gives you the tools needed to fix that dent—to heal and move on, releasing the other person for your benefit.

And do not be conformed to this world,
but be transformed by the renewing of your mind,
so that you may prove what the will of God is,
that which is good and acceptable and perfect.

ROMANS 12:2

Be kind to one another, tender-hearted, forgiving each other,
just as God in Christ also has forgiven you.

EPHESIANS 4:32

If possible,
so far as it depends on you,
be at peace with all people.

ROMANS 12:18 NASB

Father, thank You for designing us to heal,
by Your strength and power, through forgiveness.
Search my soul for dents, and walk with me as I forgive those debts.

THE BOND OF PEACE

In Ephesians chapter 4, Paul tells us to be "diligent to preserve the unity of the Spirit in the bond of peace" (verse 3). He says to be diligent, or in some versions, to make every effort. The Greek word for *bond* is *belt*. Paul calls it a peace belt. He says that you and I ought to have on our peace belt to hold up our trousers as we run after unity.

When we operate outside of God, we are automatically setting ourselves up for division. Unless we allow the Holy Spirit to rule among us as the bond that holds us together, then unity cannot be preserved or maintained. But in the power of the Holy Spirit, guided by His peace, we can stand unified for His kingdom.

With all humility and gentleness, with patience,
showing tolerance for one another in love,
being diligent to preserve the unity of the Spirit in the bond of peace.

EPHESIANS 4:2–3

Therefore from now on we recognize no one according to the flesh. . . .
Therefore if anyone is in Christ, he is a new creature;
the old things passed away; behold, new things have come.

II CORINTHIANS 5:16–17

Make my joy complete
by being of the same mind,
maintaining the same love,
united in spirit, intent on one purpose.

PHILIPPIANS 2:2

God, without Your Spirit we let the devil divide us.
But in You, we can live in peace with one another.
Help me to be a vessel of peace and to invite
You, Holy Spirit, into my relationships.

WE ALL NEED MERCY

A haughty film star went to a photographer, and after the pictures were developed, she was predictably unhappy. "Sir," she said, "this photo doesn't do me justice."

The photographer replied, "Lady, with that sour expression of yours, you don't need justice for a good photo. You need mercy."

As insulting as that joke is, it illustrates the fact that we all need mercy. Mercy assumes there is a miserable situation that needs relief. Mercy understands there are circumstances that weigh us down, and at times, we need something to come and lift off the heaviness. Mercy can be defined as compassion for people in need. It is reducing, removing, or relieving someone's distress.

When was the last time you needed mercy and received it? Or when was a time that someone's compassion would have changed your situation, but it didn't come? Each one of us is in the position to show compassion at times, and when we do, we provide hands that help to lift the heaviness of the situation. There will be consequences for actions, but mercy loves the person through it.

But God, being rich in mercy,
because of His great love with which He loved us.

EPHESIANS 2:4

He saved us, not on the basis of deeds which we have done
in righteousness, but according to His mercy,
by the washing of regeneration and renewing by the Holy Spirit.

TITUS 3:5

Blessed are the merciful,

for they shall receive mercy.

MATTHEW 5:7

_____

_____

_____

_____

_____

_____

_____

_____

_____

_____

_____

_____

_____

_____

_____

_____

_____

_____

_____

_____

God, thank You for modeling mercy.

Thank You for every time You showed me You cared about me,

even in trouble. Guide me in treating others in the same way.

GREAT LIKE A CHILD

The disciples once asked Jesus who among them was the greatest in the kingdom. And Jesus pointed to the children. He said, in essence, that if you mess with the children in any way, you're messing with Him.

The truth about children is, they're completely dependent. God says you'll never become great in the kingdom as long as you are independent from Him. Why not get in that children's ministry, that classroom, or observe your own kids, to learn how they work?

By the time kids become teenagers, it's so much harder for them to become Christians. There's a natural faith present in childhood. Allow them to be in the presence of God, in the presence of other Christians. Treat children with the utmost respect for their needs and processes.

Who are the children in your life that can give you insight into childlike faith?

Truly I say to you,
unless you are converted and become like children,
you will not enter the kingdom of heaven.

MATTHEW 18:3

Jesus said, "Let the children alone,
and do not hinder them from coming to Me;
for the kingdom of heaven belongs to such as these."

MATTHEW 19:14

All your children
will be taught by the Lord,
and great will be their peace.

ISAIAH 54:13 NIV

God, let me learn from children and not disdain them.
Give me patience to treat them with the love
and kindness that You Yourself feel for little ones.

SALT OF THE EARTH

I was at the airline club waiting for my flight one day, and a lady came and asked if I wanted something to drink. I asked for a ginger ale. When she brought me a ginger ale, she also brought something I didn't ask for: a little dish with peanuts, pretzels, and other salty snacks. I didn't ask for those snacks, but that airline club knew what they were doing! They knew that if I drank that ginger ale and ate those snacks, the salt would make me thirsty and I would want to buy another ginger ale.

You are the salt of the earth. You're supposed to be so salty in the culture that people get thirsty, and you can offer them the living water of Jesus Christ. Your job, and my job, is to make folks thirsty for Jesus Christ by how salty we are. And that doesn't happen in church, where we're surrounded by other salt in the shaker. He says we are the salt of the *earth*, where the meat is decaying and the culture is disintegrating.

How much time, and in what capacity, do you spend interacting with people who don't know the Lord but need to?

You are the salt of the earth.

MATTHEW 5:13

Whoever drinks of the water that I will give him shall never thirst;
but the water that I will give him will become in him
a well of water springing up to eternal life.

JOHN 4:14

For I will pour out water on the thirsty land
And streams on the dry ground;
I will pour out My Spirit on your offspring
And My blessing on your descendants.

ISAIAH 44:3

God, may I be just the right amount of salt
that leads others to want You.

WE'RE ALL DONKEYS

It was Palm Sunday. The young donkey was walking proudly down the road because he was carrying Jesus to Jerusalem. Everyone was waving palms as they passed, and the donkey just strutted along. The next day, the donkey got up and decided to strut down that street again. But no one came out, no one waved palms, no one shouted, "Hosanna." He went home sad, and told his mom about his disappointing morning. His mother looked at him and said, "Son, without Jesus, you're just a donkey."

With God, we don't get credit for the big things that everyone sees. We don't get credit for being famous, getting applause or accolades. We get credit for the times we touch the people around us with His love. We get credit for meeting the needs of those who can't fix their problems themselves. We do what we've been called to do, but we don't aim for celebrity status because in the kingdom, the last will be first and the first will be last, and Jesus is best.

Was there a time you did something for which you wished you'd gotten earthly credit? How did you handle it?

So the last shall be first, and the first last.

MATTHEW 20:16

But when you are invited, go and recline at the last place,
so that when the one who has invited you comes, he may say to you,
"Friend, move up higher"; then you will have honor
in the sight of all who are at the table with you.

LUKE 14:10

**Therefore humble yourselves
under the mighty hand of God,
that He may exalt you at the proper time.**

I PETER 5:6

---

*Lord, You are the best and most valuable reward.
Adjust my sight to see the world the way You do
and to love others humbly and without expectation.*

*Want more on
how to spread kindness
from Dr. Evans?*

The *Kindness in the Culture*
gift collection is coming soon
to dayspring.com and
various retail stores near you.

MERCY
is an
act
of
compassion.
—Tony Evans

kind words.
kind **works**.

KIND WORDS
ARE SWEETER THAN
HONEY
PROVERBS 16:24

called to be
kind
EPHESIANS 4:32

Be
kind
and
compassionate
to one another.
EPHESIANS 4:32

compassion
kindness
humility
gentleness
patience

Dr. Tony Evans is the founder and senior pastor of Oak Cliff Bible Fellowship in Dallas, founder and president of The Urban Alternative, and author of over 150 books, booklets, and Bible studies. The first African American to earn a doctorate of theology from Dallas Theological Seminary, he has been named one of the Twelve Most Effective Preachers in the English-Speaking World by Baylor University. Dr. Evans's radio broadcast is heard on over 1,400 radio outlets daily, and his sermons are streamed and downloaded over twenty million times annually.